HIDDEN FACES OF ANCIENT INDIAN SONG

Dedicated to all those who have helped and encouraged

Hidden Faces of Ancient Indian Song

SOLVEIG McINTOSH

ASHGATE

Published by

Ashgate Publishing Limited
Gower House
Croft Road
Aldershot
Hants GU11 3HR
England

Ashgate Publishing Company
Suite 420
101 Cherry Street
Burlington
VT 05401-4405
USA

Ashgate website: http://www.ashgate.com

British Library Cataloguing in Publication Data
McIntosh, Solveig
Hidden faces of ancient Indian song
1.Vocal music – India – History and criticism 2.Hindustani music – History and criticism
I.Title
782.4'2162'00954

Library of Congress Cataloging-in-Publication Data
McIntosh, Solveig, 1948–
Hidden faces of ancient Indian song / Solveig McIntosh.
p. cm.
Includes bibliographical references and index.
ISBN 0-7546-5104-5 (alk. paper)
1. Folk songs–India–History and criticism. 2. Folk music–India–History and criticism.
I. Title.

ML3748.M28 2005
782.42162'91411–dc22

2004012583

ISBN 0 7546 5104 5

Printed and bound by Athenaeum Press, Ltd.,
Gateshead, Tyne & Wear.

Contents

List of Illustrations

Figures

Plates

Between pages 70 and 71

Preface

Having long been interested in the sounds of North Indian music, I came to India in 1990 to try to find out something about how it is that a simple melodic phrase can be transformed into an artistic and aesthetic experience for the listener. This was a very large question to be answered and, at that time, was essentially a question about *gamaka*, the art of embellishment, tonal inflection, tonal nuance and even elements as prominent as ornaments. With this focus, the purpose of my visit to India was to interview and record as many classical vocal artists in the *khayāl* style as possible in the time available. From all these singers, too numerous to mention, I learned a very great deal.

The study of such a wide and complex subject as *gamaka* stimulated enquiry into other avenues of research so that when the study was completed what had been discovered seemed unsatisfactory. It became clear that language and music were inseparably linked. It seemed that some of the answers to the questions which had arisen lay in much older forms of Indian music, in the various systems of Vedic *mantra* recitation, in the sounds of the Sanskrit language and, if a musical style was to be part of the investigation, then it should be North India's most ancient tradition of classical vocal music, *dhrupada*. It also became clear that *how* we hear is crucial to what we hear and that this is the starting point for any enquiry. Moreover, an appreciation of underlying philosophical and esoteric concepts is essential to an understanding of the evolution of Northern India's musical tradition.

The text, preceded by an introduction, is divided into seven chapters which represent a progression from basic principles and concepts of sound and hearing to different kinds of musical composition. Some of the chapters are subdivided to enable readers to select what is relevant to their particular interests.

The Vedic tradition has shown remarkable tenacity in surviving many kinds of disruption throughout its long history. This is essentially an oral tradition and continues to be preserved as such. In this connection, of special importance in this book, is Chapter 4 on the manual gestures, the *mudrās*, which accompany recitation in a branch of the White Yajur Vedic tradition. These are illustrated by small figurative drawings and a set of colour prints.

One of the problems which arises when trying to describe what happens in Indian music and its underlying philosophy is the lack of consistency concerning the use of terminology. Some attempt has been made to address this situation both in Chapter 1 and in Chapter 6. In general I have tried to put the English before the Sanskrit terms to assist the reader who is unfamiliar with Sanskrit. The glossary may also be consulted for explanations.

Representations of musical features are given using staff notation with sharps and flats shown above the notes to which they relate. This format has been chosen to make information which is sometimes specifically about the music of Northern India accessible to a range of readers interested in world music.

Acknowledgements

The writer wishes to thank the following for their special contribution: The chapter on *mudrās* was inspired by Dr Hṛday R. Sharma, Yajur Vedin and currently Reader and Head of Department of Vedic Studies at Banāras Hindu University. I am especially appreciative of his careful explanation of the *Yājñavalkya Śikṣā* and his clear and beautiful demonstrations of the *mudrās* of the White Yajur Veda tradition (Mādhyandina Branch).

My thanks also to Dr Ritwik Sanyal, a leading vocalist in the Ḍāgar tradition of *dhrupada* singing and an academic, for some stimulating discussions about *śāstra* as well as for demonstrations of the vocal subtleties of that tradition.

A valuable contribution was made by Prā Gagādhar Deva of Banāras, in his demonstration of *vikṛti* in the Ṛg Veda tradition.

My understanding of some texts in Hindi was greatly assisted by Dr Bīna Singh Miśra who helped with translation.

Invaluable help with proofreading was given by Anne Garten and Isabelle Glover. Essential drawings were provided by Angelo Cinque.

My thanks also to the American Institute of Indian Studies for their kind permission to reproduce a photograph from their archive collection and also to the Sangeet Natak Akademi, Delhi for making it possible for me to listen to some seminar audio-tapes.

Introduction

Since the beginning of mankind there has been music. What draws us to music is a deep sense of connection with it; the laws which govern the mind and the body, the natural world in which we live and all that exists around us are reflected in the music which has been created by mankind at various times in different cultures. Music may be an attempt to express the cosmos, its order, and its rhythm; it may also be described as 'the food of love' when love does not mean sentiment, but something larger than life, more all-encompassing and at times transcendental.

In India music has never become a written art as it has in the West. Historically music often seems to have been a means of communicating essential qualities, speaking in religious and mystical terms of what could not be put successfully into words. In contrast to this trend is the preoccupation which has existed, ever since the invention of a coherent script, with the minutiae of detailed analysis which is characteristic of so much writing about sound, language and music. Concepts expounded in early texts of wisdom, the Upaniṣads, established the impossibility of capturing music too literally in a written form and teaching it too mechanically. However this has not precluded the myriad ways of trying to describe music, including its more ephemeral qualities. This is where the scientific and analytic approach has played its part so that the way in which Indian music has been explained in the various ancient treatises on music, the tradition of *saṅgītaśāstra,* may be thought of as books on the physics of sound and the theory of vibrations.

The tradition of music in India is a more encompassing concept than it is in the West; it includes a complex of thoughts, ideas and philosophy that have influenced its practice. The Sanskrit word for music is *saṅgīta*, which is a composite idea with 'song' as a central component. Song can include various traditions and styles of recitation and chant as well as composed genres. Thus the medium for the enquiry is the voice – the art of recitation and singing. Traditionally, singing has been regarded as the first art, instrumental music the second art and dancing the third art which, together, make music. This tripartite combination is a significant concept which can be found in other cultures of the world. Whether this is by coincidence or because it represents a fundamental principle, or for some other reason is open to exploration.

Science has confirmed many things which were described in treatises long ago. For instance, it has demonstrated that sound is not only audible but visible, that sound affects matter. India's seers and sages anticipated many of the insights of contemporary scientific thought, and their knowledge through experience of the higher states of the human mind continue to remain beyond the grasp of modern science. Thus it was understood that every syllable, every tone, is a vibration with a special effect; syllable and tone are inseparable although the emphasis may differ.

The ancient tradition of Vedic recitation has been preserved not only for its meaning; for some the sound of the pronunciation of each vowel and consonant, each syllable is more significant. Indeed, there are three recognised aspects of Vedic tradition: knowledge of the Vedas for their meaning alone, recitation for the sound of the *mantras* but without knowledge of their meaning and a combined knowledge of sound and meaning. The language of the Vedas, the *mantras*, together with the accents used to recite them, are the Songs of God. The importance of correct recitation of every sound, in accordance with tradition, is shown in the detailed instructions given in the phonetic manuals which belong to the different branches of Vedic tradition. If the Sanskrit language was the origin of many other languages, the origin of the science of music is also to be found in Sanskrit. Of course there have been other important melodic influences, but there are a number of ways in which components of Sanskrit language, including different styles of Vedic recitation, have subsequently influenced the musical language of India.

A considerable gap often exists between the facts of musical theory and its practice. The initial impetus for music must have come from experience, from intuition, not from theory. Just as the grammarian, Pāṇini, and other grammarians who preceded him, codified the language of the time (*c.* 600 BC), so too, at different stages in musical evolution, did the authors of the *saṅgītaśāstra* formalize the musical practice of the time. It is not irrelevant to mention Sanskrit grammar in the context of music, for an important element, which contributes to the anatomy of the music, is that its essence lies in the realm of language. Sometimes musicians themselves have been able to write about the art and science of music but this is not the usual role of the musician, even though the motivation for writing may have been inspired by the profoundly moving effect of music. Technical details are necessary, however, in order to contain the themes within the parameters of hypothesis and enquiry. Consequently this book deliberately attempts to vary between the scholarly and some more homely metaphors, between the technical and the practical, between science and poetry, so that those for whom the subject matter is new, for whom the cultural context is unfamiliar, may find at different times points of entry into the themes presented here.

The structure of this book traces a progression from basic principles of sound to different kinds of musical composition, from simplicity to complexity, from the finer concepts of sound to their incorporation within different forms of music. It first presents a context for music and musical hearing. The question of what the ear hears and how it hears is addressed. The medium for sound and hearing, *ākāśa*, is discussed and so too are the four levels of hearing, for the phenomenon of gross and subtle vibration, available to anyone who searches for it, gave rise to a profound teaching about the levels of manifestation of sound on both a universal and individual scale. This section also includes a vocabulary for expressing different qualities and aspects of manifest and unmanifest sound. As a focus for the physical approach to sound, three concepts are used: the ear, the mouth and the hand representing sound, language and gesture. Traditionally the word music (*saṅgīta*) has three aspects; one is language. The mouth, as the instrument of expression of sound, is described and examples of its capacity as a location for producing different degrees of subtlety of sound are given. This has particular reference to the Sanskrit language and mantric recitation. Chapter 3 on Vedic Accents looks at the relationship between two fundamental laws, the law of three as demonstrated in the recitation of Vedic *mantras* and the law of seven as used in various ancient ascending and descending scalar forms. The *mudrās* or manual gestures of the White Yajur Veda tradition (Mādhyandina Branch) are described in some detail. An interesting correspondence with these formalised movements are the gestures used during the slow introductory section of a *dhrupada* performance. Here the gestures may be made with the left hand rather than specifically with the right hand. On occasions both hands may be used. Moreover these gestures are spontaneous expressions made by a singer and do not conform to a predetermined pattern. However, they do illustrate the way in which gesture or movement, one of the three components of the concept of music, *saṅgīta*, pervade both recitation and musical practice. Another theme of the book outlines something of the development of early forms of music, the Vedic songs, and their development in *kīrtana*, *gītis*, *prabandhas* and *dhrupada*. Finally, the philosophical concepts of sound outlined in the first part of the book, and the various forms of scale and melody find their expression in Chapter 7, where not only musical structures are considered but also the use of the many subtle forms of tonal movement (*gamaka*).

If the starting point for this exploration is from Vedic times, with an assumed date of around 2500 BC, said to be the beginning of the Indus Valley civilization, to the present day, then this does indeed represent a very long period of musical history. But the origins of the Vedic period are obscured by time and it is really not possible to ascribe any definite dates when it is a question of the roots of very early music that have survived, handed down from teacher to disciple according to oral tradition. Historical problems and climatic conditions have obscured the preservation of the history of ancient India; the history of an art as abstract and intangible as music is even more obscure. The picture has to be pieced together from the evidence which has survived, from artefacts, documentary and literary references and from the knowledge which has been passed on through the oral traditions. In other words, it is the music itself which contains the clues, for those documents which are available today are often compilations over a period of time, representing musical practice formulated in an oral tradition. Though they may be attributed to a single author, there may have been several contributors, as they often appear to consist of historical layers and accretions, making it difficult to determine a precise sequence of thoughts and events. Just as in the field of language, where the monumental grammar, the *Aṣṭādhyāyī* of Pāṇini, is an example of the culmination of the work of grammarians and other scholars who preceded him, in the field of phonetics and music, within texts such as the *Nāradīya Śikṣā* and the *Yājñavalkya Śikṣā*, different phases of early musical history are represented.

Much of this may have been said before. After all there is ‘nothing new under the sun’ and the field of knowledge is not the possession of a single person. This book is offered as a contribution which may stand alongside the often substantial work of other writers in this field to whom the reader should also refer. Inspired by feeling, it is nevertheless a book about some of the facts of Indian music which are a necessary part of its understanding and preservation as well as its regeneration.

Chapter 1
The Ear

Hearing

I became convinced that the voice can only produce what the ear hears.[1]

What does the ear hear and how does it hear? In the history of mankind words, and particularly holy words, have taken their place in human lives not through the eye but through the ear. It has long been the practice in India to acknowledge the holiness of a word by hearing and reciting it, by participating in it. Recitation of sacred texts is considered to be indispensable to ritual practice. This practice starts with the sacred syllable *Om*. At the physical level *Om* encompasses twenty attributes or qualities, one of which is hearing (*śravaṇa*).[2] *Om* is said to be universal and all pervasive and beyond analysis. Because of this, the inference is that hearing too exists always, everywhere. The *Kena Upaniṣad* says: 'Since He is the Ear of the ear ... ' clearly stating that hearing is a condition that is always present. Individuals then have their own perception of this universal state. It is not only that the ear is the instrument of hearing, the means by which one hears, it is, as the commentary in the *Kena Upaniṣad* says, 'the organ of hearing which reveals words'.[3] In other words, it *reveals* sounds of all kinds including musical sounds. Such being the case, the element of sound, the realm of sound and the means by which sound is apprehended warrant particular emphasis in the context of the exploration of the history of musical ideas in India.

Having established that hearing is both a universal as well as an individual concept, one might ask where it begins for the individual. If one starts to answer the question from the physical point of view, then the enquiry must begin with the unborn foetus. Physiologists inform us that the ear is the first organ of the human body to be formed in the womb; when the foetus is about eight weeks old, it has all its major organs including the organ of hearing. By the ninth week the developing foetus is already hearing, already listening. Those involved with the dying tell us that the faculty of hearing is the last of the senses to be relinquished. If it is the first and the last of our existence, is it not of some special significance? As the foetus develops, important relationships between developing organs emerge. An article based on the work of the embryologist Dr Freeman elaborates the relationship between the ear, the mouth, the hands and the heart during the early stages of foetal development.[4] As will be seen in Chapter 4 this is an important concept.[5] The universe of sound in which the embryo is submerged is rich in sound qualities of every kind. After birth, the foetus has to adapt from 'liquid hearing to aerial hearing' as the outer and middle ear adapt themselves to the air around them. We can deduce, therefore, that the foetus and the baby do not hear in the same way. It is likely that the foetus hears a whole range of sounds, many of which contain low frequencies.

Why, then, is the world of sound so important? What more may be said about the significance of the ear? It is the opinion of at least one contemporary physician and physiologist that the ear's primary function is to charge the neocortex of the brain and thereby the entire nervous system. Sound is a nutrient; sound waves 'digested' by the ear provide electrical impulses that charge the brain. Dr Alfred Tomatis, an ear, nose and throat specialist, surgeon, psychologist and inventor in France, spent most of his life redefining the ear's extraordinary significance in relation to the voice.[6]

Can everybody derive benefit from sound? What about the hearing impaired, how do they obtain nutrition from sound? The answer is that the ear, that is, the outer ear, is not the sole means by which sound is absorbed. Sound waves can be perceived through the skin and bones. It is the middle ear, the bony, air-filled cavity containing the anvil, stirrup and hammer, which translates sound to the brain by whatever means it arrives. It is significant that before the existence of language in a written or visual form, the acoustic medium was not recognized as a phenomenon completely separate from the person involved in it. It was well-known that through the sense of hearing the life-current (*prāṇa*) touches the five senses: the sense of sight, the sense of hearing, the sense of smell, the sense of taste and the sense of touch. For a person does not only hear sound by means of the ears alone; sound permeates his entire being. In this way it can affect the metabolism, the circulation of the blood, the nervous system and bring about a change in mood. It has to be remembered that one writes at a time and in a culture that is dominated by the visual form. At other times aural domination has been much more typical of some non-Western cultures and of cultures existing at a different time in history. It is not surprising therefore, that studies of thought in early India make it clear that the subject of sound was something to be taken seriously and the idea of sound as a nutrient is not a new idea, as the study of at least one phonetic manual (*Yājñavalkya Śikṣā*) and its related *Brāhmaṇa* reveals.

Why is man fitted with two ears? The joke sometimes made is that man has two ears but only one tongue so that he can listen twice as often as he speaks. But this, as has been observed, is not actually the case as 'we do not have one tongue but two joined together by the median'.[7]

Why this duality in the design of the human body? How does each individual ear function? Examination of the organ of hearing reveals a veritable miracle of engineering in the realm of human evolution. The ear consists of three parts; it has an outer construction and an elaborate inner construction. Any external sound, such as speech, recitation or music, creates molecular energy and the energy patterns that are created are translated into the brain. Thus, when an event outside the physical body takes place, creating waves of vibrational energy, these waves are collected by the external part of the outer ear (*pinna*) and concentrated into the auditory canal which extends approximately 1¼ inches into the head. They travel along the auditory canal to the ear drum which is a membrane about ¼ inch in diameter and 1/300th of an inch thick. These sound waves cause pressure on the ear drum so that it begins to vibrate and in so doing sends its vibrations into the middle ear. The function of the outer ear, shaped like a spiral, is to 'catch' vibrations travelling through the air. One has only to cup the ear in one hand, and extend the scope of the outer ear as a sound deflector to appreciate the purpose of this external construction.

The second part of the ear, the middle ear, is a small cavity filled with air and surrounded by very dense bone. It is said that this bone is the densest in the whole human body. Air comes into the cavity of the middle ear through the back of the throat, through the Eustachian tube. When the outside air pressure changes, for instance when travelling upwards in a lift or changing altitude in an aircraft, the pressure on the ear drum is equalized to prevent distortion of the ear drum. Resembling a bony bridge through the middle ear there are three small bones (ossicles) which are all connected to each other and referred to as the hammer, the anvil, and the stirrup. The hammer is connected to the middle of the ear drum and moves as it moves, the anvil connects the hammer to the stirrup, and the stirrup transmits the sound vibrations to the entrance of the inner ear. The role of the ossicles is to act as an intermediary system which transfers the sound vibrations from the outer ear to the inner ear.

The inner ear is a bony labyrinth consisting of two major parts, the cochlea, which looks like a very small snail shell ¼ inch in diameter at its open end, and the semi-circular canals. While the semi-circular canals are connected with equilibrium rather than with hearing, the cochlea is a spiral tubular structure in the inner ear which converts sound energy into nerve impulses. This spiral construction is filled with fluid called perilymph. Resembling a partition between the upper chamber and the lower chamber, as if floating in the perilymph, is another membrane, the basilar membrane. The basilar membrane runs along the length of the tube and vibrates when sound is conducted to it from the ear drum. Vibrations through liquid are much stronger than through air. It is estimated that along this membrane there are as many as 30,000 hair cells arranged in rows and approximately every five hair cells are connected to a nerve fibre or neuron. It is also said that each of the 30,000 hair cells has between 12 and 40 hair cilia protruding from it. The process of hearing takes place when the sensitive cilia are stimulated to respond to the movement of the fluid in the cochlea, exciting the hair cells, which in turn stimulate the neurons, which transmit the vibrations along the auditory nerve, through the temporal bone into the brain. The work of the cochlea is to translate a distribution of frequency into a distribution of space; different parts of the membrane respond to different frequencies, and this results in the corresponding area of the auditory cortex of the brain being excited. The area near the base of the cochlea is more sensitive to higher frequencies; the area near the apex of the cochlea is more sensitive to lower frequencies.

The 'oval window' is between the middle ear and the start of the cochlea's chambers; the other chamber is separated from the middle ear by the round window, a thin membrane which vibrates with the movement of the perilymph. At the far end of the cochlea both chambers meet at a small opening in the basilar membrane called the helicotrema. As sound vibrations agitate the stirrup, the oval window moves inward, and since the fluid within the cochlea is incompressible and contained by the bony shell-like structure, the round window responds to the fluid by moving outward.

Low-pitched sounds travel the entire length of the cochlea, cross the basilar membrane near the helicotrema, and go back to the round window. Higher pitched sounds do not travel as far along the basilar membrane before returning to the round window. There is a point along the basilar membrane at which the vibrations cross over and it is thought that at this point electro-chemical impulses are created affecting the appropriate neurons which send the sound messages to the brain.

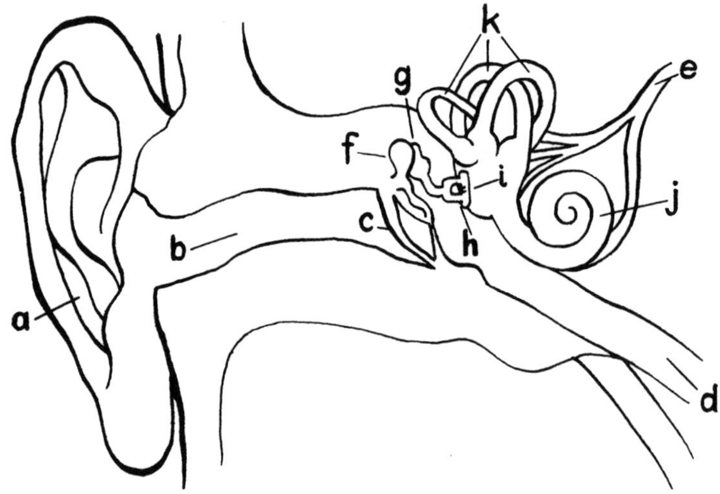

a.	outer ear	h.	stirrup
b.	auditory canal	i.	oval window
c.	ear drum	j.	cochlea
d.	Eustachian tube	k.	semi circular canals
e.	to the brain	l.	basilar membrane
f.	hammer	m.	helicotrema
g.	anvil	n.	round window

Figure 1.1 Cross-sectional diagram of the human ear

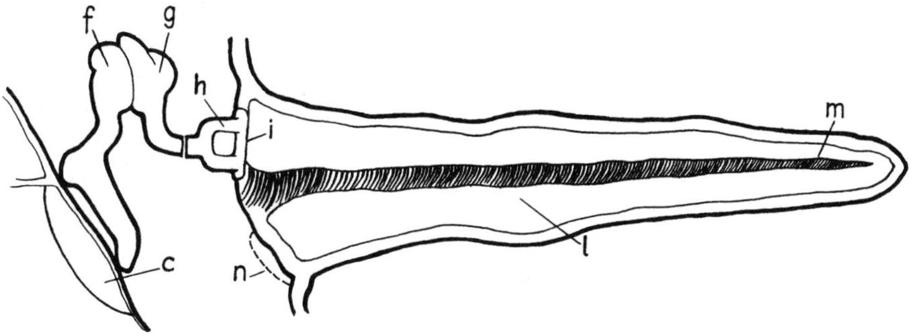

Figure 1.2 Cross-sectional diagram of the middle and inner ear

How, then, does this highly complex organ, consisting of several different structures working simultaneously, connect with the brain? Sound messages reach the brain at the thalamus situated just above the brain stem. This is where sensory input is integrated and related to the appropriate area of the cortex. The thalamus relates to the limbic system which, although not fully understood, is believed to contribute to emotional response to performing or hearing music.

This is the journey of sound from its source, through the medium of air, into the three parts of the ear and into the cerebral cortex of the brain which is its final destination. This physiological process is common to all members of the human species regardless of race, or cultural considerations. All sounds within the environment follow this path, though it has to be remembered that only a portion of these sounds reach the level of our conscious awareness. Human hearing only responds to a fraction of the available range of vibrations in the physical realm.

This discussion needs to be extended further because there are different levels of hearing, much finer levels of audition. In other words, there is a hierarchy which in turn relates to a neurological hierarchy. For example, there is sound which cannot be heard at the physical level, but which is apprehended by the 'yogic mind' as part of its experience. The 'yogic mind' is not a state which occurs only in those who have become recluses in the Himalayas, but exists for any individual regardless of geography. To take this idea further one should consider the teaching on the four energies of sound (the *śaktis*) and the concept of *nāda*.

We return to the question as to why we have two ears? Could we make sense of sounds, and in particular musically organized sounds, with just one? We hear binaurally and although to outward appearances the two ears appear to be the same, the roles of the right and the left ear are very different; there are internal structural components which account for this. The right ear usually dominates operations because it processes information more rapidly. 'It is the larynx which presents a lack of symmetry, and it is this lack of symmetry which reflects in some way the lack of symmetry of the ears.'[8] A parallel situation exists in the mouth, to which we will refer in Chapter 2. But what exactly happens? At the physical level, the passage of the nerve impulses, via the recurrent laryngeal nerves belonging to the tenth cranial pair (pneumogastric), from the cortex to the lining of the left larynx, is longer than that from the cortex to the right larynx. This results in a greater proximity in the relationship of the right ear to the organs of speech. Experimentation shows that the hearing process of the right ear comprises five main stages: right ear, auditory centre of the left brain, central laryngeal motor area of the left brain, speech muscles, and the passage from mouth to right ear. The left ear, however, comprises six stages as sound travels to the auditory centre of the right brain. The theory is that to reach the central laryngeal motor area (which is situated in the left brain) a transfer of the left brain centre is necessary; this transfer constitutes an element of delay, which can be measured, and this delay varies, according to the individual, between 0 and 0.4 of a second.[9] Contemporary psychological research also confirms different roles for the right and left ear. Experimentation revealing aural paradoxes suggests that the right and left ears, which are primarily linked, respectively, to the right and left hemispheres of the brain, prefer different areas of the spectrum of pitches. The left ear favours lower notes, the right higher ones.[10]

Current medical research compares interestingly with ancient sources of explanation. In the *Yājñavalkya Śikṣā*, a phonetic manual compiled in written form during the early years of the first millennium, a descriptive quality is given for the right ear. It is described as having the quality of 'going with speed', further explained as having the ability to 'catch the quality of the sound quickly', whereas the left ear is described as having the quality of 'storing the energy of sound'.[11] It is for this reason *mantras* are often given by the initiator into the right ear of the initiate. The *Nāradīya Śikṣā*, a phonetic manual relating to *Sāma Veda* recitation, also specifies that the seven *svaras* (tones) should be sung into the right ear of the student as it is in this way that the treatises (*śāstras*) are to be passed on from the teachers (*ācāryas*) to the students (*śiṣyas*).[12]

Hearing is not always the same activity as listening. Different types of listening can change the posture of a listener. In response to music some listeners begin to hold themselves more upright with their head slightly bent forward, while others manifest a quickening or a slowing of their heartbeat. In fact, the ear imposes a wide range of impressions on the body. While such observations tend to reflect the findings of the empirical scientist, it has been observed in the realm of esoteric philosophy, in the context of Vedic recitation of *mantras*, that the intention of the chanter affects his physical posture. One Vedic priest from the tradition of *Yajur Veda* observed that when Vedic recitation takes place on the occasion of some sort of public display and the ceremony is very long, the body may easily become slumped as recitation proceeds. Not so when the recitation takes place in a more private setting, for example in a temple, and it is dedicated to the divine. Then the spine is inclined to straighten quite spontaneously without any specific thought or intervention on the part of the reciter.[13]

At the physical level, it can be appreciated that the ears and the hearing system represent a very exceptional system within the body. It is an interesting evolutionary observation that, unlike the eyes, there is no mechanism for closing the ears in the same way; the concept of 'earlids' does not exist. There is, however, a compensating device for screening out unwanted sounds, but it operates in the psychological rather than the physical domain. Selective hearing takes place when our attention is focussed in a particular way or when we tune into something with a related frequency level. In a culture, a Western culture, dominated by the visual image, the vital role of sound and the auditory system becomes forgotten, but it is this system which not only gives us something as basic as our sense of balance but also has a special role to play in memory, as well as emotion. Cultivation of memory through the faculty of hearing is much neglected in the West but was and continues to be considered essential for many processes of learning in India. Its roots lie in the origins of the oral tradition, before the invention and use of written forms, as a way of passing on and preserving knowledge. This applies to knowledge of the sacred scriptures as well as to music. We can even go so far as to say that the average western mind is defective in this area, through lack of exercise. We could, however, increase our everyday capacity for an awareness of the world of sound in which we live by asking such simple questions as, 'How many birds have you heard today?' and 'What was the first sound you heard this morning?' This practice begins to change the level of alertness.

It is said that 'The voice translates and betrays the functioning of the ear'.[14] The relationship between the activity of hearing and the activity of speech is important. It is important on different levels. At the physical level, hearing precedes the production of sound whether through speech or song. Contemporary research shows that the inability to utter a particular phoneme may well be because it has never been heard. This observation is echoed in the Indian musical *śastraic* literature by Abhinavagupta, a tenth-century philosopher and commentator on a much earlier work, the *Nātya Śāstra* compiled by Bharata around AD 200 and considered to be the most important of the early treatises on music. In praise of the virtues of practising the *vīṇā* (a long-necked, fretted stringed instrument) as an aid to singing, he says, 'Thus, one who cannot produce the notes through his voice, due to being unable to comprehend a particular note in his mind, can easily render these notes on the *vīṇā*'.[15] Any student of a musical culture which is foreign to them will have had some experience of this situation; they will have encountered the effort necessary to produce, vocally, the particular nuances of that musical language which lies first of all in the requirement that the sounds be experienced aurally. They should be able to *hear* the sounds required and, depending on the style of music, this may be more than a question of physical hearing alone. A spectrum of sound requires a corresponding spectrum of hearing.

Sound and Space – *Ākāśa*

All the religions have taught that the origin of the whole of creation is sound.[16]

Sound and the potential for manifest sound, and therefore expression and communication of all sorts, resides in potential at the level of *ākāśa*. This is the medium of sound. It is the element which records permanently all that ever occurs anywhere in the cosmos, like a 'great memory'.

> *Akasha* is the first among the five elements and has been accepted in the majority of the systems of Indian Philosophy as being all-pervading, indivisible and devoid of accumulation or aggregation. It has been described as a 'free or open space, vacuity, the ether, the subtle and ethereal fluid (supposed to fill and pervade the universe and to be the peculiar vehicle of life and of sound).[17]

Ākāśa is an intermediary stage between *Brahmā* the Creator, the presiding deity of any one universe through which the multifarious forms of this world find their way, and Earth which is the ultimate stage of manifestation. Its position therefore is pivotal. It is described as *setu* (a bridge) or 'transformer' of energies or 'interpreter' having in potential the qualities of both sides, the manifest, the coarse physical world, and the unmanifest, the world of subtle and causal nature. It is due to *ākāśa* that creation comes into existence, for it has the quality of sound and through sound all comes into being. This universe is said to be based on sound. So the idea gives a certain significance to sound, the way we perceive it and therefore our relationship to the world we live in.

In a progression from *Brahmā* to Earth, from unmanifest to manifest, from fine to coarse, the next stage of manifestation after *ākāśa* is *vāyu*, usually translated 'air'. But it is a larger concept than the air we breathe. Philosophy and scientific thought meet in a description of *vāyu* as a 'field', a 'field' in which the human body operates, a field which includes the universe, the sky, the earth – in fact, everything one can see. *Vāyu,* then, can be said to be associated with different fields of energy. This might also include the field theory of the body whereby every organ of the body is understood to be a coherent field pattern. The next state of manifestation is *tejas* or 'fire'. Fire in this context is often translated as 'form' and this interpretation can include all levels of form right down to the atomic or particle state, the state of ions. Similarly the next state, *āpaḥ*, translated as 'water' encompasses the liquid molecular state in general. The final stage of *pṛthivī* or 'earth' is the solid state reflecting the qualities of all the previous stages, each element containing within it the previous one. As the *Taittirīya Upaniṣad* says:

> From that Brahman indeed, which is this Self, was produced space. From space emerged air. From air was born fire. From fire was created water. From water sprang up earth. From earth were born the herbs. From the herbs was produced food. From food was born man.[18]

The scheme describes accumulating levels of density, from *Brahmā* to man, with *ākāśa* as an important intermediary step.

Western scientific thought includes in a perspective on the nature of *ākāśa* or space, the idea of fields outside ordinary perceptions of time and space in which all events are recorded, a sort of genetic account for future generations to draw from and add to, to learn by. Before this twentieth-century formulation, physicist Michael Faraday, writing in the nineteenth century, hypothesized that a person's actual boundaries are established, not by the physical body, but by the extent to which one's influence is felt. Modern science has also discovered that the impression of sound on material substances can be made clearly visible.[19] Different impressions that have been made by sound have been seen in the forms of leaves and flowers and other natural objects. It follows from this that hearing can impose a wide range of impressions on the body. This supports the belief expressed so often in ancient literature that the first manifestations of the creative source were audible before they became visible. It has even been said that 'one reads with one's ear.'[20] So, everything which we see around us in the world is the phenomenon of sound. Therefore, according to the theory of fields, there is a field in which all the music ever played reverberates – a field into which musicians pour their own music so that they expand the field just as much as they are enriched by it. This, of course, includes music of all cultures.

The *Bṛhadāraṇyaka Upaniṣad*, which is said to be the oldest and is certainly the longest of the principal Upaniṣads, presents an expansive vision of the cosmos. The upper, middle and lower levels represent the three aspects of time – past, present and future – which are 'woven' across *ākāśa*, while *ākāśa* itself is permeated by the 'unseen Seer, the unheard Hearer, the unthought Thinker, the ununderstood Understander'. These eight verses are an important expression of this concept; many of the Upaniṣadic teachings can be found in seed form within the *Bṛhadāraṇyaka Upaniṣad*.[21]

If *ākāśa* is 'the audible space that fills the universe' from which grosser substances are derived, it is easy to appreciate the importance given to all that is inherent in the power of sound and hearing with its manifestation in speech and music. The *Chāndogya Upaniṣad,* which is related to the Songs of the *Sāma Veda*, says:

> Wherefore do all these worlds come? They come from space, and into space they return: space is indeed their beginning, and space is their final end.[22]

In the same Upaniṣad it states that the light which shines beyond this heaven, beyond the whole creation, beyond everything, is the same light that shines within a person. To perceive that light it is the faculty of *hearing* to which one appeals. The connection between speech and light is frequently made in the Upaniṣads. One should close the ears and 'hear directly in this way a sound like rumbling, like bellowing, like that of burning fire. That which is such is to be meditated on as seen and heard'.[23]

The *Maitri Upaniṣad* expresses the same idea:

> ... by closing the ears with the thumbs they hear the sound of the space within the heart. Of it there is this sevenfold comparison: like [the sound of] rivers, a bell, a brazen vessel, a wheel, the croaking of frogs, rain, as when one speaks in a sheltered place.[24]

The science of speech and phonetics gave the first description relating to sound production and manifestation; it was within this context that the concept of musical sound was expounded. The phonetic manuals (*śikṣās*) are evidence of this, instructing those who recite the *mantras* of the Vedas on correct pronunciation, the underlying purpose being the attainment of a changed state of consciousness.

While these early manuals relate to Vedic and Upaniṣadic literature, later Yogic and Āgamic (Tantric) sources arose during the seventh century AD, and described a relationship between syllabic sound and musical tones within the context of *cakras* (wheels, cluster points). The petals of the different lotuses representing the *cakras* carry specific letters of the alphabet. The letters of the alphabet are arranged throughout the *cakras*, starting with the *mūlādhāra cakra*, at the lowest point and culminating in the *ājñā cakra* at the brow. According to this system, the seven syllables (*svaras*) are placed on the petals of the *viśuddha cakra* and the sixteen vowels (*mātṛkā*) are located on the same *cakra*. Vowels have particular characteristics which are not applicable to consonants, such as pitch and duration. These characteristics also apply to tones. Although the letters are concerned with syllabic sound whereas music is concerned with tonal sound, the inseparability of syllable and tone is well recognized in Indian thought even though there is a difference of emphasis. It is reflected in many examples throughout Indian literature pertaining to music. The use of the word *svara* for both vowel and tone indicates their close association with one another.

The affinity between music and yoga is one of the many systems which emerged for describing a hierarchy of sound in general and musical sound in particular. Although a later (thirteenth-century) account given in the *Saṅgīta Ratnākara* is understood to be taken from yogic and tantric literature, it shows significant differences. The musical aspirant is advised to start concentration on the heart, leaving the three 'lower' centres, for it is in the heart, the meeting place of earth and space, that the movement towards *ākāśa* starts. The three centres most relevant to musical expression are said to be the heart, the throat and the back of the neck. The gateway to supreme bliss and immortality is the *sahasrāra cakra*, the thousand-petalled lotus *cakra* situated above the crown of the head. Consequently, concentration on this centre is strongly recommended in this treatise. Earlier schemes, such as those used for the recitation of the Vedas, tend to emphasize the navel for the focus of attention and indeed the explanation given of *nāda* includes this centre. The basis for the selection of certain focal points by the authors of the *Saṅgīta Ratnākara* is not entirely clear. Although this is a later system for describing the movement of sound than that referred to in the earlier Upaniṣads, it nevertheless continues the theme of describing relationships between sound and different points in inner space. It also includes the possibility of transcending inner space and the physical realm, to arrive at a space of pure consciousness. Space whether inner or outer, is *ākāśa*. As the *Kena Upaniṣad* states, 'He is the Ear of the ear' indicating that a person's capacity for hearing is but an instrument for universal hearing which resides at the level of *ākāśa*.[25]

The relationship between sacred sound and music is well known to those familiar with Pythagoras and his teachings on the Harmony of the Spheres. This Western school of thought associated the sacred aspect of music with the sacred qualities of numbers and ratios, whereas the Indian tradition bases this same idea on the divine nature of sound and the word. This is an important distinction. While every musical system starts from the same impetus, described in the Indian philosophical system as *Om*, it can be seen that two streams of influence have been at work in what we know of the earliest stages of the evolution of Indian and Western music.

> Words are the Vedic Yoga: they unite mind and matter. Pure, ecstatic contemplation of phonetic sound reverberating on the ether in the sacred chant may be compared to the contemplation of geometrical forms and mathematical laws by the Pythagoreans. The Word is God, Number is God – both concepts result in a mind of intoxication.[26]

Although it would not be inappropriate to question the impetus for these two streams of influence, when tracing the early developments in Indian music, it is the 'Word' to which one must turn.

The Ear of the Heart – Levels of Sound

He who knows the secret of the sounds knows the mystery of the whole universe.[27]

The investigation of sound was perhaps the single most important impetus for study among the ancient seers and sages of India. These early scientists repeatedly experimented and observed sound in different realms of experience with a persistence and passion that cannot be ignored. The first written description of sound available, and therefore an important starting point for an exploration of the subject, occurs in the *Ṛg Veda*:

> catvāri vāk parimitā padāni
> tāni viduḥ brāhmaṇā ye manīṣiṇaḥ
> guhā trīṇi nihitā nengayanti

turīyaṁ vāco manuṣyāḥ vadanti[28]

Four are the levels of speech.
The wise who possess insight know them all.
Three levels, hidden in secret, cause no movement.
The fourth is the level that is spoken by Mortals.

If hearing precedes speech, as has been discussed previously, this verse could just as easily be referring to four levels of hearing. This phenomenon of gross and subtle vibration is available to anyone who searches for it and explores it, and those who discover it may be reassured that the great esoteric and spiritual traditions have also studied it. In India it became a specific science often referred to as 'the science of *mantra*'.

A profound teaching evolved about the nature of sound and its relationship to life. In brief, sound-energy can be described as passing through three successive stages or levels, also referred to as four energies or vibrations (*śaktis*) of sound, each stage being a progression from the previous level, with the fourth stage being the ultimate manifestation. This theory of four levels of sound, though usually referred to in the context of speech, has a cosmological aspect for it is also a description of how the universe becomes manifest.

Descriptions of the fourfold partitions of speech and their relationship to the universe also occur in the Upaniṣads. The most notable example is the *Māṇḍūkya Upaniṣad*, said to have been in existence from around the seventh century BC though it could be much older than this. This Upaniṣad relates the sounds *a*, *u* and *m* to the three states of waking, dreaming and deep sleep or, to use another formulation, to the physical, subtle and causal levels. These are the levels through which the individual soul passes when moving from its ordinary state to union with the fourth state, *brahman*. This Upaniṣad thus makes a connection between sound and levels of consciousness, there being three states with a fourth state which transcends all three.

Apart from the very early reference to levels of sound manifestation which occurs in the Ṛg *Veda*, originally heard by the seers and sages (*ṛṣis*) and therefore not chronologically accountable, another early formulation of the theory of three stages of speech (*trayī vāc*) is to be found in the first books of the *Vākyapadīya* by Bhartṛhari, a grammarian writing around the middle of the fifth century AD. The formulation of this theory is likely to be earlier than Bhartṛhari, but there is no evidence to prove how ancient it may be. Although the much quoted hymn of the Ṛg *Veda* (1.164.45) had already distinguished four forms of speech (*vāc*), and although there had already been speculations in the Upaniṣads about the four partitions of speech and their correlation with the universe, this was an important formulation of a principle which describes three levels of apprehension in human consciousness, namely *paśyantī*, *madhyamā* and *vaikharī*. Whatever the exact origins of the theory, it was a particular feature of Tantrism, and notably in non-dualistic Kashmir Śaivism where the clearest explanation can be found.[29]

Bhartṛhari's theory was followed by Somānanda soon afterwards (*c* AD 875-925) who postulated a fourth and 'ultimate' stage, thus completing the formulation already set out in the *Ṛg Veda* many thousands of years previously. But this is not a remote idea belonging to an equally remote culture during an almost inconceivably distant time. While not wishing to trivialize the profundity of this theory, its universality can be discovered by anyone in any culture who delves deeply enough into experience through media such as poetry or musical composition.

In outlining these four levels of speech or sound, the question is whether the process should be described as starting from gross physical sound and traced to its origin, or the other way around. We probably think we relate to what is most familiar and accessible, outward speech. Consequently a left-hemisphere speech-centred approach might appear to be the best way to approach this investigation, but in truth the process is the other way around, with speech being the final outcome of the progression.

The understanding which science has today, that vibration is at the heart of the whole of creation, was a certainty to people living thousands of years ago. It was the basis of scientific thought in the *Ṛg Veda.* The sounds that these mantric rhythms articulate are the vibrations taking place at four levels of being or manifestation, from the absolute state, transcendent, unaffected by anything and said to be contained in the sound *Om*, the causal sound (*praṇava śabda*) for our creation. From this sound have come into existence all words, all forms and objects. This level is referred to as *parā*.

The next aspect of sound in the progression from unmanifest to manifest, is that of *paśyantī*, a word which has its root in the Sanskrit word 'to see'. This state is an ambiguous condition in that it represents a transition between a state of complete lack of differentiation and the commencement of differentiation. It is the causal state where meanings are universal and at the same time it is the stage where the inner vision takes place; it is the level of pure vowel sounds, where the *mantra* or seed sound is perceived by the seer. Another aspect of this state is where mind and *prāṇa* (life force or breath) unite enabling vibrations to manifest.

Although the four states are often referred to as levels there is nothing which divides one state from another; each merges with the other. Consequently the location of *paśyantī*, with reference to the human form, can be said to be in the region of the navel where it manifests as a vibration having the quality of 'a single spark'. Here it is described as being like a seed, a single conscious vibration (*spandana*) which only the Self knows. But it can be said to relate to the heart centre as well, where it may be described as a point of confluence, the place from which one can comprehend everything, for it is in this place, in the heart, that the invisible realms, that form the unconscious impulses for our thoughts and actions exist. It is the place of *aham*, the pure Self, and it is the region where the vowel (*svara*) sounds, which are 16 in number and referred to as *mātṛkā*, are held. These are the 16 energies (*śakti*) of the Absolute and it is from this level of causal sound that all words, including *dhātus* (roots in Sanskrit from which words are derived) first come into being.[30]

Paśyantī, conceptualized as that which is 'seen', implies the concept of 'light' for how can vision, whether inner or outer, take place without light in some form? 'Seeing', in this context, is not a literal idea involving the physical eye, but is an expression used when dealing with the non-material world, perceived by the 'inner eye'. It is said that at this level the 'illumined Word' occurs when an underlying truth or archetype is perceived; as its nature is light it manifests as revelation. Revealed sound may be heard with the outer ears as external music, but there is another music, a divine music, which is heard with the 'ear' of the soul. Thus it is the place of the 'eye' of the heart and the 'ear' of the soul, the capacity which the soul has for 'inner seeing' and 'inner hearing', where the two experiences are not separate as they are at subsequent levels. It is the level at which the Creator may be first 'heard' or apprehended, in the form of the most beautiful music, the divine music, the Music of the Spheres.

The third level of manifestation of sound is called *madhyamā*. This is still an intermediate stage as its position is between the undifferentiated state (*paśyantī*) and manifest articulated speech (*vaikharī*). Again it is not the ears which register this level; it is apprehended through the mind. It is abstract and yet its meaning is fully comprehended by the individual. It is best described as a mental state where concepts are formed into separate thoughts, where there is linguistic consciousness of phonemes, words and sentences. With reference to Sanskrit grammar, it is the third stage which precedes the spoken word, the level at which noun stems (*prātipadika*) are conceived. At this stage too comes rhythm. In terms of individual consciousness, this is the stage where the mind becomes aware of its own capacity for speech. Thinking deeply about something or wondering about ideas leads us into this state. Most artistic and creative thinking comes from this level; it is the level where musical inspiration is given form before it is manifest in sound. The spoken word, the poem, the song is merely the end product of a provisional stage during which the ear, in its own way, already rehearses what is going to be pronounced. Mind, ear and larynx become connected. Therefore it is the level which stands as a bridge between the inner, private and subjective realm and the outer, manifest forms of sound. Thus it relates to the heart but also to the throat or larynx as the breath and sound-current engage and prepare for the state of audible sound. Later stages of esoteric teaching, namely Kashmir Shaivism around the ninth century, connect each of these stages to the unfoldment of a *cakra*. This is a general term which means 'wheel' or 'circle' and refers not only to energy centres of the body, but also to collections of forces which in turn relate to the sounds of the alphabet. This is a complex and sophisticated exposition which traces all manifestation back to a single root sound.

The fourth stage is that of *vaikharī* which is said to be in the throat, the mouth and the tongue. The concept of 'mouth' often includes the throat. Although *vaikharī* is the level of manifest, audible speech, it is only an instrument which reflects the processes which have taken place at the previous three levels. The original sounds emerging from *Om* (*AUM*) are in one state, whereas those uttered by the mouth are in a completely different state, having reached the end of the process. Is it possible to believe today that at one time this original sound was the only sound needed by mankind! In its most limited form *vaikharī* operates mechanically, reiterating conventional meanings of words or clichés. It can be said that this form of the spoken word is the final result of a provisional stage during which the 'ear' has rehearsed what is going to be pronounced. However, audible speech is not entirely limited to the mundane level for it can reflect the qualities of the previous three levels described, depending on the calibre of the speaker. Musical articulation is subject to the same limitation as speech; one can be aware when a musical rendition is mechanical, when it lacks inspiration and does not seem to 'come from the heart'. Contrary to this there are those precious moments during a musical rendition when, although the music is operating in the sphere of physical sound, the heart is 'touched by stillness'. At these times the connection has been made with the inner realms.

According to different systems of philosophy there are further subdivisions of these four main divisions of sound. Thus there would seem to be a hierarchy of sound although in truth there is no separation between the levels. The subtlest level incorporates the densest level. There is also the concept of *nāda brahman*. It too is a concept which describes successive gradations of sound, of musical sound in particular, both manifest and unmanifest, inspired by the vital energy which permeates the entire universe. Everything depends on the capacity for hearing. Just as a single bird singing in the midst of a city's rush-hour traffic will not be heard, so too will subtle vibrations not be heard amidst the noise of the untrained mind.

Words for Sound

In the Sanskrit language there exist many words for 'sound', each attempting to capture various subtle shades of meaning. There is also the tendency in Sanskrit to use the same word in a general as well as a specific sense. Overlapping meanings may be represented by the same word; for example, the word *svara* may refer to a vowel, a syllable or a musical tone. Although there is a difference of emphasis between these three manifestations of sound, the use of the same term (*svara*) nevertheless indicates a proximity of meaning. Some other terms for sound are: *dhvani*, *śabda*, *śruti*, *sphoṭa*, *vāc* and *nāda.* Each term embodies a world of meaning which has given rise to much detailed discussion. A summary of these meanings will be given here.

Foremost among the words for sound is *Om*, the most prevalent sacred sound and symbol for the mystery of the divine. The word *Om* which we pronounce with the throat, mouth and lips is not the ultimate sound (*nāda*) which manifests in the Absolute (*Brahman*). It is a representation of that ultimate sound which cannot be uttered through our physical vocal organs. In its physical form it is often referred to as *praṇava śabda* or *praṇava Om* (*Brahman* with attributes). Sometimes referred to as *akṣara* with the sense of a syllable which is 'imperishable' and later known as *oṁkāra*, it first appears in the Upaniṣads. The *Māṇḍūkya Upaniṣad* expounds on the three sounds *a, u, m*, of which it consists. Interestingly, the syllable *Om* is not mentioned in the *Ṛg Veda*. It is first named in the *Śukla Yajur Veda*.[31]

Vāc, personified in the Vedas as the goddess of speech, is often associated with the Saraswatī, goddess of speech and music portrayed holding a *vīṇā*, representing a feminine principle.[32] It has a range of meanings relating to speech such as, 'to say, utter, announce, proclaim, recite and describe'. Goddess Saraswatī is very ancient in Indian conceptual thought. She is embodied in the great river named after her. Bringing divine sustenance and nourishment, she can be considered the patron of deities within the ancient Vedic civilization. Later she became associated with speech and music and with recitation, chant and song.

Sphoṭa is derived from the root '*sphuṭ*'. The dictionary definition includes the meaning 'to burst' and has the sense of opening, expanding or blossoming and at the same time conveys the idea of sound as eternal, indivisible and creative.[33] As a sound in the form of a word, it represents an idea which 'bursts or flashes on the mind when a sound is uttered'. The *Dhātu Pāṭhaḥ* in fact gives two sets of meanings but, as far as music is concerned, we may say that *sphoṭa* is an indivisible entity whereas *dhvani* are those sequences of sounds which are uttered in order to manifest *sphoṭa*. Musically it has the sense of a sound which bursts open and blooms as a flower does. The terms *āghāta* and *anuraṇana,* meaning 'struck' sound or the onset of sound and the resonance which arises from this attack, are associated with this concept as is the relationship between *śrutis* and *svara*. These are inseparable relationships which Mataṅga observed in a set of five poetic and penetrating observations. The *śrutis*, for example, become transformed into *svaras* just as milk is transformed into curds and whey.

Dhvani as a musicological concept has more of the sense of resounding or reverberating with such meanings as, echo, noise, voice, tone, tune, thunder, and even the sound of a drum.[34] Patañjali the grammarian, whose writing has been dated around 200 BC, says that it is *dhvani* that makes sound audible. In the *Bṛhaddeśī* of Mataṅga, written approximately AD 800, it is referred to as the ultimate origin of all creation, analagous to *śabda brahman* or *nāda brahman.*[35] *Dhvani*, he says, shines in the form of the letters of the alphabet. The term which is used for the alphabet as well as for vowels and syllables is *svara*. This word can be derived with reference to two verbal roots, *svar* meaning 'to shine' and *svṛ* 'to sound'. Thus *svara* descending from *dhvani* is of the nature of sound and light.

Śabda is a widely used term in contemporary parlance having a general meaning, sound and noise, and a more specific musical meaning, tone or note.[36] Indian grammarians have used the word *śabda* to indicate a sound which has meaning while phoneticians have used the term *nāda* to signify the 'voiced' sounds of vowels, as contrasted with the 'unvoiced' sound of most consonants.

Critical to later discussions on the nature of sound, those that arose around the ninth century with the development of Kashmir Shaivism, is the concept of *spanda*. The word has the sense of throbbing or pulsing and as such refers to that impetus which arises as a wave out of the ocean of Consciousness. It is an impulse to create which comes not only from the centre but from everywhere at once so that from *spanda* the whole world comes into being. It is like a resonance, an interplay of vibrations from which the world of matter comes into existence. In this way matter comes from vibration, an idea which corresponds with the findings of contemporary scientific thought. Quantum physics has concluded that everything is a form of energy, that the seemingly solid particles of our physical world are formed by the intersection of waves of energy. Sound and movement are one and, because the esoteric texts refer to much subtler vibrations as well as to the gross sounds we are more familiar with, we can conclude that those texts and the scientists of today are likely to be describing the same thing.

Śruti is a popular term in contemporary musical parlance implying a range of meanings. It is a term which has given rise to much discussion and research among both Indian and Western scholars. The word is derived from the Sanskrit root *śru* 'to hear' and refers to 'that which can be heard'. The number of *śrutis* in an octave is generally stated to be 22 but the reason for this continues to be a source of debate. The concept of *śruti* is inextricably related to that of *svara* (tone). Probably the earliest reference to this relationship is to be found in the *Nāradīya Śikṣā*:

> The *śruti* in a music note is not visible like the way of a fish which moves in the water or the birds in the sky.[37]

The same source mentions five *śrutis* in relation to the Sāmavedic scale which describe tone quality rather than precise measures of pitch. In the *Nātya Śāstra* attributed to Bharata-Muni, dated between 500 BC and AD 200, *śruti* are mentioned in connection with the *grāma* (tone systems) in use at that time and also in the context of *alaṅkāras* (musical figures). A commentary on the *Saṅgīta Ratnākara*, the most frequently quoted Sanskrit treatise on music, thought to have been written during the thirteenth century AD by Śārṅgadeva, says:

> It seems that historically the perception of *svara* is prior to that of *śrutis*, and that the concept of *śruti* was necessitated for an adequate apprehension of tonal phenomenon.[38]

Other schools of thought argue that the musical notes (*svaras*) take precedence and that it is only the presence of *svaras* that enables us to perceive *śrutis*. While often referred to in terms of interval measurement, the seven *svaras* being separated from each other by two, three or four *śrutis*, it is not so much a linear concept but more a way of referring to subtle differences between one audible sound and another. Scientific research during the last 30 years has found that the function of the inner ear (organ of Corti) is more complex than previously thought. The auditory mechanism does not only convey the main tone, but also its partials as well as summation and difference tones. The human brain has the faculty, as previously described, to convert this complex stimulus of the ear nerve into a tonal unit, called main tone, while still distinguishing its components. The outer landscape of the physical phenomenon and the inner landscape of the psychological perception are different. At one level *śruti* appears to be a linear representation of a complex non-linear phenomenon. In yet another sense the word *śruti* refers to that which is apprehended by the *ṛṣis* (seers); the Vedas, it is said, were not man-made.

The discussion about sound is not complete without special mention of *nāda*, causal sound, the undifferentiated absolute as *nāda brahman*. There are two explanations for the derivation of this term: the system according to grammarian Pāṇini gives the root *nad* meaning 'to sound, thunder, roar or howl' and has the sense of a sound which reverberates loudly, while according to Nirukta, an older method of analysis, the two syllables, *na* and *da* symbolize *prāṇa* and fire respectively.[39] The latter explanation is also favoured in a much later work the *Saṅgīta Ratnākara.*[40] Language constantly evolves. An older form of language than that expounded by Pāṇini existed and so too has an older form of music. Thus *nāda* is a generic term for a concept of sound which is a basic element of music and an important idea underlying traditional Indian thought. The term is not used in the *Nāṭya Śāstra* of Bharata (*c* AD 200); probably the earliest reference to this concept occurs in the *Bṛhaddeśī* of Mataṅga:

> Now, I speak about the principal definition of *nāda*.
>
> There is no *gīta* (song, music) without *nāda*, there are no *svaras* (musical notes) without *nāda*, there is no *nṛtta* (dance) without *nāda*, hence the world is of the essence of *nāda*.
>
> Brahmā is known to be of the form of *nāda* (*nāda-rūpa*), Janārdana (Viṣṇu) is of the form of *nāda, Pāra Śakti* is of the form of *nāda* (and) Maheśvara is of the form of *nāda*.
>
> That which is spoken of as the location (*Sthāna*) of Brahmā and which is known as *brahma-granthi, prāṇa* is seated in it, *vahni* (fire) arises from *prāṇa, nāda* is born of the combination of *vahni* (fire) and *māruta* (air).
>
> From *nāda* is formed *bindu* and from *nāda* all *vāṅmaya* (whatever is made of speech or language) (is born).
>
> This is the opinion of some (authorities).
>
> The air arising from the location of *kanda*, (and) moving about up and down, produces the intense course of *nāda*.
>
> So say others.
>
> The letter '*na*' is spoken of as *prāṇa* (air) and the letter '*da*' is known as fire; this is spoken of by me as the meaning of the dual verbal component (*pada*) of *nāda*.

> This (word) *nāda* is derived from the *dhātu* (root) *nadati* (to make inarticulate sound) and is fivefold viz. *sūkṣma* (subtle), *atisūkṣma* (very subtle), *vyakta* (distinct) *avyakta* (indistinct) and *kṛtrima* (artificial).
>
> The *sūkṣma* (subtle) *nāda* dwells in the *guhā* (lit. cave, secret place) the *atisūkṣma* (very subtle) one in the heart, the distinct one in the throat, the indistinct one in the *tālu* (lit. palate, but here cerebrum) and the artificial one in the region of the mouth; thus should the fivefold (*nāda*) be known by the wise.

He concludes:

> Thus I have spoken about the beautiful origin of *nāda*.[41]

This passage, which is often quoted, is a useful summary of several theories of sound, expounded 'in a charming way'. It is interesting because it makes the connection between *nāda brahman*, music and the Hindu deities and reinforces existing concepts of sound in terms of gradations of emerging vital energy. This is a formulation of the process and the motivation by which the eternal, unmanifest principle underlying sound is articulated in the material world. The desire of the Self, the *ātman*, to utter sound and communicate gives rise to speech and song. The way in which this concept developed in different philosophical schools has led to considerable intricacy of thought.[42] It seems clear that Mataṅga was influenced by Tantric philosophy and he is the first author to introduce these details. Thus the tradition of *nāda* yoga overlaps with the tradition in *Saṅgīta Śāstra* of mentioning *cakras* as found in both Yoga and Tantra systems of philosophy. Probably influenced by Mataṅga, the *Saṅgīta Ratnākara* contains an entire section on *nāda brahman.*

> We worship *Nāda-brahman*, that incomparable bliss which is immanent in all the creatures as intelligence and is manifest in the phenomenon of this universe.[43]

The way in which sound is manifest in the human body is then described:

> Desirous of speech, the *ātman* (*jīva* or individuated being) impels the mind, and the mind activates *agni* (the battery of power) stationed in the body, which in its turn stimulated *prāṇa* (vital force). The vital force stationed around the root of the navel, rising upwards gradually manifests *nāda* in the navel, the heart, the throat, the cerebrum and the cavity of the mouth as it passes through them.[44]

There follows a fivefold description of *nāda* which is reminiscent of a description given by Mataṅga:

Stationed in five places, *nāda* takes on five different names as associated with them respectively, viz. *atisūkṣma* (extremely subtle), *sūkṣma* (subtle), *puṣṭa* (strong), *apuṣṭa* (not-so-loud) and *kṛtrima* (modified).[45]

It is also reminiscent of an earlier work, the *Nāradīya Śikṣā* where five qualitative attributes of *śruti* are given:

One who does not know the distinction between the *śruti-s* viz. *dīptā āyatā, karuṇā, mṛdu* and *madhyamā* is not recognized as a teacher.[46]

Subsequent verses describe how these *śrutis* relate to the *sāma svaras*. While it is not easy to decipher an exact meaning for these verses, it nevertheless seems clear that the pitches of the Sāmavedic chant were to be invested with particular tonal or timbral qualities.

Thus *nāda* is understood to be of two kinds: unmanifest or 'unstruck' (*anāhata*) and manifest or 'struck' (*āhata*). Both occur in music and can be heard by the trained ear. Consequently, there are those who say that *nāda* is of two types, spiritual and musical. The concept of *nāda* as a basic element of music is an important idea which connects with the concept and use of *śrutis* and is a term which is used in a variety of ways.

Notes

1 Alfred A. Tomatis (1991), *The Conscious Ear: My Life of Transformation Through Listening,* Station Hill Press Inc. New York, p. 53.

2 The root given for *Om* is *ava.* Its attributes are listed in the *Dhātu Pāṭhaḥ*, an ancient dictionary consisting of 2000 roots with their meanings. See the 1984 edition edited by Professor J.L. Shastri, p. 12.

3 *Kena Upaniṣad* with the commentary of Śaṇkarācārya, translated by Swāmi Gambhirananda, 1.2.

4 Freeman, 'The Human Embryo's Use Of Its Self', p. 63.

5 Fertman, 'The First Sound', vol. 2, no. 6, p. 17.

6 Tomatis gives an account of his work in his book, *The Conscious* Ear: *My Life of Transformation Through Listening.*

7 Tomatis, p. 50.

8 Tomatis, p. 50.

9 Tomatis, p. 51.

10 Researched by Diana Deutsh, Professor of Psychology at the University of California at San Diego and cited by Paul Robertson, *Music and the Mind*, BBC Channel 4 Television, 1996, p. 8.

11 *Yājñavalkya Śikṣā*, 1:24.

12 *Nāradīya Śikṣā*, 1.8.5.

13 An observation made to the writer in 1999 by Dr Hṛdaya R. Sharma, Reader and Head of Vedic Studies, Banāras Hindu University.

14 Tomatis, p. 53.

15 Mukund Lath (1978), *A Study of Dattilam*, Impex, Delhi, p. 17.

16 Hazrat Inayat Khan (1977), *Music*, Samuel Weiser, New York, p. 8.

17 Monier-Williams, p. 126.

18 *Taittirīya Upaniṣad* with the commentary of Śaṇkarācārya, translated by Swāmī Gambhirānanda, 2.1.

19 Hans Jenny (1974), *Cymatics. Wave Phenomena, Vibrational Effects, Harmonic Oscillations with their Structure, Kinetics, and Dynamics*. Basilius Presse, Basel, Switzerland, vol. 2.

20 Tomatis, p. 89.

21 'Bṛhadāranyaka Upaniṣad' 3.8.3-11, in Hume *Thirteen Principal Upaniṣads*, pp. 118-119.

22 'Chāndogya Upaniṣad', 1.9.1, in *The Upanishads*, Penguin Books, New Delhi, trans. Mascaró.

23 *Chāndogya Upaniṣad*, with the commentary of Śaṇkarācārya, translated by Swāmī Gambhīrānanda, 3.13.8.

24 'Maitri Upaniṣad', 6.22, in Hume.

25 *Kena Upaniṣad*, trans. Swāmī Gambhīrānanda, 1.2.

26 Richard Lannoy (1971), *The Speaking Tree: A Study of Indian Culture and Society*, Oxford University Press, London, p. 276.

27 Hazrat Inayat Khan (1972), *The Sufi Message*, 2nd edn. Barrie Rockcliff, London, vol. 2.

28 *Ṛg Veda*, 1.164.45.

29 For further discussion see Guy L. Beck, *Sonic Theology, Hinduism and Sacred Sound*, Moltilal Banarsidass Publishers Pvt. Ltd. Delhi, p. 163.

30 Sanskrit verbs are traditionally identified by their root followed by the third person singular, present active indicative form.

31 *Śukla Yajur Veda*, 2.13.

32 Speech is feminine in gender but writing is said to represent a masculine principal and left-brain function. See Leonard Shlain, *The Alphabet and the Goddess*, 1998.

33 Monier-Williams, p. 1270.

34 Monier-Williams, p. 522

35 See the *Bṛhaddeśī of Mataṅga Muni* c AD 800, ed Prem Lata Sharma, published in Indira Ghandi National Centre for the Arts, *Kalāmūlaśāstra* series 1992, 1.1-13.

36 Monier-Williams, p. 1052.

37 Nārada, *Nāradīya Śikṣā, with the Commentary of Bhaṭṭa Śobhākara*, 1.6.16.

38 Shringy (1972), 'The Concept of Sruti as Related to Svara – A Textual and Critical Study', *Journal of the Madras Academy*, vol. XLIII, pp. 111-128.

39 The *Aṣṭādhyāyī* (Eight Meditations) dated around 600 BC and attributed to Pāṇini represents the culmination of the work of preceding grammarians. It formalized the Sanskrit language. This work was succeeded by Kātyāyana's examination of the Sūtras and subsequently by the commentary of Patañjali in his *Mahābhāṣya*,

'Great Commentary'. In linguistic history the Nirukta is also a well-known work, the oldest existing Indian treatise on etymology, philology and semantics, codified by Yāska. It contains the Nighaṇṭus which are glossaries of rare and obscure words occurring in the Vedic hymns. The philosophy of this method maintains that every sound has significance and derives the meaning of words from *bīja* (seed) syllables.

40 Sharma, and Shringy (1991), *Saṅgīta Ratnākara of Śārṅgadeva*, vol. 1, Munshiram Manoharlal Publishers Pvt. Ltd., New Delhi, p. 113.

41 *Bṛhaddeśī of Mataṅga Muni*, 1.17-23.

42 André Padoux (1992), *Vāc. The Concept of the Word in Selected Hindu Tantras*, Sri Satguru Publications, Delhi, pp. 96-105.

43 Sharma, and Shringy, vol. 1, p. 108.

44 Sharma and Shringy, vol. 1, p. 111.

45 Sharma and Shringy, vol. 1, p. 112.

46 *Nāradīya Śikṣā*, 1.7.9.

Chapter 2
The Mouth

Architecture of the Mouth

> *The voice is not only audible, but also visible, to those who can see it; the voice makes impressions on the ethereal spheres, impressions which can be called audible but are visible at the same time. On all planes the voice makes an impression, ... Other sounds can be louder than the voice but no sound can be more living.*[1]

Why place such emphasis on the mouth? As has been explained in a previous chapter, *vaikharī* is the last stage of the manifestation of sound at the physical level and this takes place by means of the mouth. The Indian concept of manifest or audible sound, whether in relation to Sanskrit language or to music, focuses primarily on vocal sound. Musical instruments such as the *vīṇā*, conch, flute and drum are referred to in ancient literature, but they are not given the same status as the voice which is considered the paradigm for instrumental music. This particular role of the voice has been acknowledged and described in a variety of noteworthy contexts. The *Taittirīya Upaniṣad* states that meditation on the body should consist of the juxtaposition of four aspects: the lower jaw, the upper jaw, the tongue which is the link between them, and speech, the meeting place. Meditating in this way will result in a range of benefits.[2] The commentary on the *Kena Upaniṣad* says that 'speech is the organ which, clinging to eight localities, viz. the chest, throat, root of the tongue, teeth, nose, lips and palate and being presided over by Fire, expresses the letters'.[3] Six of these seven localities relate to the mouth, including the throat which is considered part of the mouth in terms of articulation of sound.

Thus the mouth is an instrument of expression and the language to which the above description relates is the Sanskrit language. But what is this language? Sanskrit is said to be 'well-created' or 'perfectly-made' speech, the highly evolved language of the gods. It is derived from the prefix '*sam*' meaning in this instance, 'well', the augment '*s*' and the root '*kṛ*' meaning 'to do, make, perform, prepare, undertake'.[4] It is said to have come with creation and as such is pure and clean and can mirror the laws of the universe. Sanskrit has another name, *Devavāṇī* or 'language of the gods'. It is said that divine knowledge should be recorded, written and spoken in a divine language. Certainly it can be seen that more spiritual teachings as well as works on metaphysics and mythology, poetry, drama and philosophy have been written in Sanskrit than in any other language.

The Vedas, which are four in number, represent the sacred books of the ancient religion of India. (The word '*Veda*' may also be used to refer to the four Vedas together with the body of literature which has gathered around them.) Sanskrit is considered to be the language of the Vedas. It originated from the *ṛṣis* or seers of the Vedas and Sanskrit was created out of the Vedas. It manifests from the divine word *Om* ॐ It has been explained that this is the causal word for our creation out of which all words, all forms and all objects have come into existence. Out of this word came the vowels and then the consonants. A special quality of vowels is that they resonate at three levels of anatomy: the physical level, the subtle and the causal or spiritual level. Many cultures believe in the importance of vowels. In the Indian tradition they are called '*svara*', which means that which exists by itself, and the consonants are called '*vyañjana*', which means that which shines. So it is that the vowels constitute the Will of the Absolute through which the creation is being regulated, and the consonants are part of *prakṛti* (creation). Just as *prakṛti* cannot work by itself but must have the support of *puruṣa* (the Creator), so the consonants must have the help of the vowel sounds. Thus a consonant cannot exist by itself. No consonant can be spoken without a vowel but together they form words. These are natural words which are not created, only experienced and seen by Realized men. Some such words are very specific in their use. Just as there are technical words used in law, medicine and other special branches of study, so there are certain words which are used only for spiritual work and not for ordinary communication.

It can be seen that there are two ways of talking about Sanskrit and its connection with other languages. One way is linguistic, finding common elements in, for example, prefixes used in Greek and Sanskrit. The other approach is the philosophical one where it is understood that all languages originated from one language – *nāda Brahman.* From this there follow the four energies of sound, *parā*, *paśyantī*, *madhyamā* and *vaikharī*, as have been described already. In brief, *parā* is the level of pure silence where meaning cannot be formed into words. It is the level of pure consciousness. *Paśyantī*, the causal world, is the state where mind and *prāṇa* are joined and vibrations begin to manifest. *Madhyamā* is the subtle level where sound related to knowledge is formed into separate thoughts. It is at the fourth stage of *vaikharī* that the mouth is involved, thus making sound audible to the human ear. Worldly communication is materialized in this state.

For worldly affairs artificial words are created by men. In this connection it is interesting to note that Sanskrit may be the root of the greatest number of languages in the world including the main languages of Europe, North India, Iran and the Middle East:

> The Sanskrit language is the basic language in the world, the prime language, the first language, and it is the purest of all languages. In the course of time, all other languages have evolved from Sanskrit; one can find from an ordinary dictionary that the English language has plenty of Sanskrit words, so have other languages, in India and abroad.[5]

However, in these forms language does not have the same potential for the inner world of a being as the original language does.

There is another reason why Sanskrit is called 'well-created' and this is because it can affect all the energy points of the body. This again makes it different from other languages. Traditional science describes the effect of Sanskrit in this way, while contemporary science talks in terms of building neuronal bridges between the two brain hemispheres, bringing them into alignment and consequently leading to balance in life. It has also been said that:

> When a sound with its measures of vowel comes to be uttered, it creates a particular type of vibration and these vibrations affect the outer creation and also the inner metabolism of the individual. This works at physical, subtle and causal levels.[6]

For matter which appears to be solid substance can be saturated and charged with sonic energy because, in truth, there is no such thing as matter, only finer and finer subatomic particles which, at a certain stage, are no longer particles but become wavelengths or vibrations constituting the basic energy waves of creation. So it is the combination of vowels and consonants arranged in a particular way that creates this vibration which can lead to true peace and happiness.

But how is this potential to be realized? Sanskrit's unique quality has to do with the way the sounds are structured and where they are located in the mouth. First of all every letter of the alphabet can be learned as a resonating energy. This requires knowing the five basic positions of the mouth and the different sounds which can occur at each position. Awareness increases the resonating potential of the sounds. When chanting Sanskrit, the phonetic manuals (*śīkṣā*) describe in detail how the mouth is to be prepared and how sounds are to be uttered. The reason for such specific instruction is that an energy system underlies recitation and it is important to know how to keep the current of energy flowing. Every combination of sound follows precise laws of harmonics. It is a language where numerous small particles coalesce in such a way as to create the most euphonic blending of letters into words, prose and verse. There is much to be gained from chanting with correct sound pronunciation even when the meaning is not known as it brings a sense of contact with the divine which is always present. One can learn the alphabet and chant *mantras* without ever going on to learn the language, although undoubtedly the experience deepens when more of the meaning is understood.

In this way one could say that Sanskrit is a science of sound, or even a vibrational grammar, as much as it is a language. It grew out of the language of *mantra*, the original form of language where sound and meaning correspond. Such language belongs to Vedic literature. This is a language where meaning is intimately connected with the divine; the force of the sounds, which reflect the intrinsic vibrations behind all objects existing in the phenomenal world, is directed towards the ultimate Sound or Word. Moreover, it is said that the Vedic language of *mantras* is not man-made, but occurred to the seers in a flash. However, the evolution of language is like a river; it flows relentlessly from its source. So, there came a time when there was the need for a grammar or system to regulate the flow. Such a system was Pāṇini's monumental work on grammar (*c.* 600 BC) which has been claimed as a summary of the grammarians of the age and time. This set of grammatical laws which relate to universal laws, was compiled in the *Aṣṭādhyāyī*, a collection of nearly 4000 axioms (*sūtras*). This is just one of the ways of studying the laws of Sanskrit grammar so that it is possible to understand how Sanskrit is formed from first principles.

Thus there are different ways of learning Sanskrit and there is very much more that can be said on the subject, but ultimately, Sanskrit is a language which exists for the sake of the Self. As both the *Māṇḍūkya Upaniṣad* and the *Bṛhadāraṇyaka Upaniṣad* state in one of the four great utterances (the *mahāvākya*), 'This Self is the Brahma' (*ayam ātmā brahma*).[7]

However, the purpose of this chapter is to make the connection between the organ of articulation, the mouth, and the medium in which it operates, for the utterance of sounds has its effect on the ether (*ākāśa*), different sounds giving rise to different vibrations. For practical evidence of the effect of sound on matter consider the work of Hans Jenny.[8] Such work shows how the impression of sound falls on objects, remains for some time and then disappears. As the form of every sound is different, it follows that every vowel, every consonant, every syllable that is uttered through the mouth has a special effect. It affects each cell and atom of the body with which it resonates. Those who study the Vedas may not study the meaning alone; Brahmins may study the pronunciation of each sound, each syllable, each word. It is their life's work because it is said that a thousand repetitions will one day create a particular magnetic energy. A hundred thousand repetitions ensure that it stays for ever and survives death.[9]

Therefore it is not for any trivial reason that clear instructions are given in such treatises as the *Yājñavalkya Śikṣā* regarding care and preparation of the mouth for recitation. These are not meaningless rituals nor are they simply social conventions of the time. They show us that there has existed a special awareness of the mouth as the organ which strongly influences sound vibrations, that interior dome-shaped cavity which is instrumental in causing sounds to resonate.

The commentary on the *Yājñvalkya Śikṣā* says that cleaning the mouth should take place in the morning before talking. Small sticks of particular trees should be chewed so that the juice is extracted.[10] The Indian Materia Medica gives these trees as the mango tree, *Butea frondosa* (the wood apple tree whose three leaves are traditionally used in the worship of Lord Siva), *Achyranthese aspera* and the acacia tree. Another verse (*śloka*) gives the names of other trees which are rich in sap. Using the wood from these trees brings 'sweetness' to the recitation.

Awareness of different potentialities of the mouth is likely to have been greater at one time than it is today. We usually assume we have two ears but only one tongue. But this is not actually the case; we do not have one tongue but two joined together by a median, as the experience of dental anaesthesia clearly shows. If we have not already observed that we have two mouths, a 'right' mouth and a 'left' one, again dental anaesthesia can make this clear. It is a situation which mirrors the two hemispheres of the brain referred to in Chapter 4 on hand gestures (*mudrās*). Although the left area of the brain may be generating the sentences, we need the co-operation of both sides of the tongue, as well as the lips and vocal chords, in order to speak. We may also observe, though most of us probably have not, that under normal circumstances our mouths contain four octaves of teeth, two on the upper jaw and two on the lower.

The subject becomes yet more interesting when one considers the acupuncturist theory that there are two acupuncture systems within the mouth, the tongue representing a whole system of diagnostic points just as the ear does, or indeed, other parts of the body. It is a hologram.[11] The relationship of the tongue to the roof of the mouth in *mantra* recitation is a very specific one. Moreover, if the information given in the *Yājñavalkya Śikṣā* is to be believed, we are given another interesting function of the tongue. 'The Vedas,' it says, 'should be learned by rote. When they are practised a hundred times and then again revised a thousand times, they will remain permanently on the front portion of the tongue for, just as water flows downwards and forms a pool and remains there, so knowledge flows to the front portion of the tongue and stays there.' Thus the body stores memory.[12]

Already we can sense that the mouth has an architecture. The Sanskrit language makes specific use of five different areas of this architecture, this gateway into the inner rooms and corridors of sound. The throat, the palate, the roof of the mouth, the area just behind the teeth and the lips all have the articulation of certain sounds associated with them. Some sounds use a combination of locations. Aspects of the architecture of the mouth may be static but within this interior cavern much movement takes place. The interaction of the tongue and upper palate is a highly sensitive relationship. The upper palate has been discovered to have a system of 84 meridian points specific for certain sounds, and when touched in the right combination and sequence, can create certain effects.[13] Anyone who has explored the instructions given by Pāṇini for the pronunciation of Sanskrit will have discovered that it is the whole tongue and not just the tip that stimulates these points.[14] The theory is that these points of sensitivity within the mouth are related to the hypothalamus which is situated close to the palate bone and can be affected by vocal sounds.[15] In this respect the thalamus and pineal gland may also be involved. When a resonance on the upper palate is produced, a frequency of vibrations creating a field of fine energy related to the energy field of the universe may be brought about. In this way the activity of the tongue and palate have the potential for raising the level of consciousness. *Mantra* recitation is designed for this purpose, as the authors of the *śikṣās* relating to the major Vedic traditions have explained. Their explanations could be reworded using contemporary idioms for it is as if we exist rather as a television does in relation to a remote control. We are the remote control which can connect with the universal set at another level when the vibrations of the control and the set match each other. This was the work of the ancient seers who designed *mantras* which have the potential to create vibrations in us which resonate with other levels. Put in scientific language, it can be said that the individual creates a frequency of vibration within his electromagnetic field which interacts with the electromagnetic field of the cosmos. The ancient texts describe what happens, for it is said that:

> There is a channel called the Sushumnā, leading upward, conveying the breath, piercing through the palate. Through it, by joining (*yuj*) the breath, the syllable *Om*, and the mind, one may go aloft. By causing the tip of the tongue to turn back against the palate and by binding together (*sam-yojya*) the senses, one may, as greatness, perceive greatness.[16]

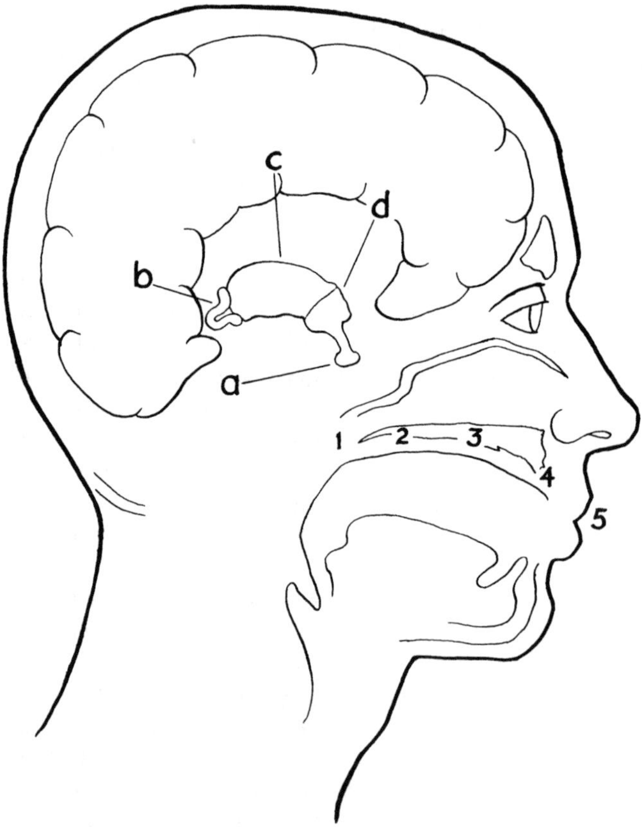

a. pituitary gland
b. pineal gland
c. thalamus
d. hypothalamus

See Appendix 2 for sounds produced at Positions 1–5

Figure 2.1 Pronunciation of Sanskrit sounds and glands in the brain

Language, Music and Dynamics of the Mouth

> *The mantras of the Vedas are remarkable in that they bring blessings to the world in the form of sound – even if the meaning is not understood.*[17]

It has been said that the first sounds which mankind made to express thoughts and feelings were in the form of vowels – 'the whole human race was at that time of one language and of one lip.'[18] It is also known that there exists a language which is for yogis and only for communicating on matters directly related to God, referred to as '*sandhya bhasha*'[19] For more varied as well as mundane levels of communication, language has been classified into three types, 'isolating', 'agglutinative' and 'inflectional', the last being the most highly developed and occurring in Aryan and Semitic tongues. What a vast time-span is implied in these few observations.

Sanskrit is an ancient language, a root language.[20] The *Aṣṭādhyāyī* (Eight Meditations) attributed to the grammarian Pāṇini around 600 BC is a codification of the language of the time. Interestingly, it seems that a great turning point in the cycle of our present humanity came about around this date, during the time of Pythagoras, Confucius, Gautama the Buddha. The *Aṣṭādhyāyī* is evidently the culmination of a long and sophisticated grammatical tradition and reveals how the language of the educated priestly class had diverged from that of the sacred hymns. The language which Pāṇini so thoroughly dissected and described was not principally the language of the Vedas but the language of contemporary educated speech. The *Aṣṭādhyāyī* shows how Sanskrit is developed from first principles, how each word is built up from a root, how innumerable small particles of sound come together to form language. This exposition in the form of *sūtras* shows how, according to laws, an initial idea or impetus in the form of a root or *dhātu*, expands to become a fully inflected word.

A similar process of expansion from an initial impetus or tone to a complete musical expression can be found echoed in expositions of *rāga*, especially during the *ālāpa* stage of performance, revealing an intimate connection between language and music. A twentieth-century Indian musicologist observed that, indeed, Indian music does consist of innumerable small structures which coalesce.[21] A similar idea has been expressed by Raghava R. Menon: 'Another element which contributes to the autonomy of the music of the *rāga* is that its essence lies in the realm of language.' Unlike the Western system 'the ground of *rāga* is language …'[22] That language starts with the concept of syllable, a sound phenomenon to which any number of transitory or ornamental qualities may adhere.

The period around 600 BC seems to have been an epoch-making time, for not only was the existing language codified, resulting in what is now referred to as classical Sanskrit, but similarly there emerged a new type of music, known as *gāndharva*. Just as classical Sanskrit had its roots in Vedic language so too did *gāndharva* music have its origins in Vedic music, in *sāmagāna*. Like the Vedic music this form of music was also considered sacred. As happens when significant changes take place, something is gained but at the same time something is usually lost. The codification of classical Sanskrit resulted in the loss of some characteristics and subtleties of an older language, that which was used in *mantra* recitation. The evolution of music is likely to have followed a similar pattern.

The first indications, however, of a connection between language and music are recorded in the earliest known sources of linguistic and musical history. In the *Ṛg Veda* there is a hymn to knowledge, attributed to *Bṛhaspati*, the Lord of the Word, which recounts the origin of sacred speech and cautions:

> Many a man who sees does not see the Word
> And many a man who hears does not hear it.
> Yet for another it reveals itself like
> A radiant bride yielding to her husband.[23]

Similarly, we will never hear this music, nor any of the music of the Indian tradition, if our ears are full of the sound of Mozart or Strauss or any other of the giants of the Western musical tradition. For this reason the sonority of Vedic recitation, the medium for expounding such words, may not enrapture us at first because of our present-day cultural conditioning, but it is through recitation that such words of knowledge and wisdom are given added strength and vitality. The sound of the spoken word can have great force in this form. Such ancient music, when we are able to tune ourselves to it, can give rise to a powerfully felt inner resonance with an accompanying sense of stability and harmony. Not only is this due to pronunciation of the language of the hymns but it is also due to the special use of rhythm and time. This ancient science of music is often referred to as *mantra* yoga. It is a language which enjoyed a greater flexibility than does classical Sanskrit and can be seen manifested in the Vedic hymns, the songs of the *Ṛṣis*, those inspired poets of a far-off time.

Svara

These early beginnings in India's musical tradition centre on the use of the voice. Although there is historical evidence for the use of instruments such as a *vīṇā* and flute, it is the voice which is the substance and paradigm for India's music. Just as in language *svara* means vowel, so in music a single unit of the scale is the *svara*, a concept which is not the same as that of the note in the Western system of music. *Svara* is both a name and a quality which manifests through the human voice and, it is argued, cannot be reproduced by any other means, however sophisticated the technology. Consequently, direct comparison with the notes of the scale as used in Western classical music is not possible, for the relationship between *svara* and note is one of impression rather than one which can be quantified mathematically and is more appropriately referred to as tone. *Svara*, it is said, when rendered by a master musician has a transcendent, ephemeral quality for those who can hear it. For this reason attempts to capture Indian music in notation have to be seen in perspective; it is a device which is useful in the same way that reductionist science is useful but there is an aspect which eludes captivity in the symbolism of written notation.

Thus the discussion about *svara* as musical tone is said to start in the realm of language. This is where a definition for the term *svara* emerges. The term can be traced to the Sanskrit root *rañj*, 'to be coloured, to glow', to which has been added the prefix *sva* denoting 'self'.[24] *Svara* is, therefore, that sound which has the capacity to glow on its own. It also has the sense of becoming illuminated and of delighting, all of which interpretations have been used at different times. Indeed, the grammarian Patañjali refers to *svara* as *svayaṁ rājante* or 'self-luminous'.[25] This same idea can be found embedded in concepts which apply to music. It is not confined, however, to a single tone. The earliest indication of this can be found in the hymns (*sāmans*) of *Sāma Veda* recitation where the term '*svara*' is as likely to refer to a musical phrase or motif as it is to an isolated tone. In this context it is a word which encompasses the idea of a movement or a vibration of sound. An early musical work, Nārada's *Śikṣā*, which pertains to the *Sāma Veda*, describes five tonal qualities. Complementary to this is the *Nātya Śāstra* of Bharata which speaks of *lakṣaṇas*,[26] finesses integral to a tone or *svara*. The fact that they are mentioned so specifically in this work confirms the idea that a tone could and should include an inherent quality of unusualness. Both references indicate that such musical concepts in the Indian tradition are of considerable antiquity.

A single sound may have very little meaning for most Westerners. The idea that a single tone can have sufficient 'substance', that it can have musical value and stand or 'glow' on its own, may seem strange but this is what musicologists much later, such as Mataṅga writing in the ninth to tenth century, were trying to clarify. They tried to describe the relationship between *svara* and *śruti* (audible sound). Mataṅga presented his point of view in characteristic philosophical terms illustrating the relationship between *śruti* (meaning simply 'that which can be heard') and *svara* in five different ways.[27] Of those five he favours the view that *svaras* manifest as a result of *śrutis* in the same way as objects, such as a pitcher, placed in the dark are revealed by the light of a lamp. In other words, although light does not bring things into existence, it does enable cognition and perception of what already exists in darkness. Thus *śrutis* reveal *svaras*.

Abhinavagupta, the great tenth-century Kashmiri Shaivite philosopher and commentator, reasons otherwise. It is tone (*svara*) which has the inherent quality of charm and musical appeal with *śruti* dependent upon *svara*, for *svara* has the quality of resonance (*anuraṇana*). The intervals of the octave in the Indian system have many possible gradations; they are much more finely graded than the Western system of major and minor intervals. It was argued that only intervals separated from each other by a certain measure (of *śrutis*) gave rise to a quality of resonance which could be called *svara*. *Svara*, therefore, came to have a twofold meaning; in association with the root *rañj* it has become associated with *rāga* or melodic form, while at the same time its etymological definition implies various qualities of emotional arousal.[28] Consequently, *svara* is understood to mean that sound which, dependent on the laws of acoustics, resonates on its own, creating emotional appeal or delight in the listener and, at the same time, is the basis of organized melodic structure. *Śruti* does not have this capacity. This view is echoed later in the thirteenth century in Śaṁgadeva's much revered musicological work the *Saṅgīta Ratnākara*:

> Immediately consequent upon *śruti*, creamy and resonating, the sound that delights the listeners' minds by itself is called *svara*.[29]

Apart from the several footnotes pertaining to the translation from Sanskrit which are well worth reading in this edition of the *Saṅgīta Ratnākara*, it is interesting that Saṁgadeva in his definition of *svara* has departed from the linguistic connotations of 'light' and 'shining' referring to the emotional aspect of the root *rañj*, 'to delight', emphasizing that the element of resonance, or beauty of tone, depends on the ratio of resonating (*anuraṇana*) and unresonating (sometimes referred to as *āghāt*) sound present in its production.

While such qualities may be inherent in a musical tone or *svara*, they nevertheless have to be cultivated in those who wish to produce such sounds. A properly produced tone (*svara*) has a sense of dimension. The significance of *svara* is such that there is in the Indian tradition of music a system for changing the state of a person which is not the same kind of work as usual musical practice and is undertaken for different reasons. It is based on a technique known as '*svara sādhanā*' (disciplined practice of tones). The result of *svara sādhanā* is not the same as having a good voice or being a good performer, but it does require devotion. It is not easy work because it requires solitary work on the tones of the musical scale, but it is the means whereby a particular element or subtle quality can enter the singing voice and allow *bhakti* or devotion to shine through. It is said by some that the power of the tones is the secret of singing, for example, *kīrtana*, because this '*svara*' is a quality which hides within the musical note. This invites the question as to whether *doh* of the Western solfa system is the same concept as *Sa* of the Indian *sargama* system. Can it be said that a *ṛṣi* or a yogi are the same as any other person just because they have similar bodies?

Nasalization

There are more hidden subtleties to be discovered than the practice of *svara* alone and it is to Vedic Sanskrit and the language of Vedic recitation that one has to turn for further understanding. Take, for example, the idea of nasalization which is described by Pāṇini in his grammar and dealt with so specifically in that manual of phonetics, the *Yājñavalkya Śikṣā* and its commentary. A dry subject one might presume until some kind of experience brings the whole thing to life.

There are various ways of talking about nasalization. In all ordinary words there is an element of nasalization; if someone has a cold and the nose resonance is blocked it is easy to hear that sounds do not have the proper resonating quality. Similarly with singing. This is the first level of nasalization. It is an external level.

Philosophically, it is said that there are two proccesses in creation: explosion or separation (from the Source) and fusion (return to the Source). The original purpose of nasalization was to take one back to the Source. There is always some level of nasalization in *sandhi* (junction point), even in a situation where a dental sound meets a palatal sound.[30] The particular effect of nasalization depends on its association with other centres of energy in the body. Recitation which takes place in *pada pāṭha*, where the words are separate, does not create the same effect as *saṁhitā pāṭha*, where the euphonic uniting of separate words, according to the laws of *sandhi*, has taken place.[31] In *pada pāṭha* the connection is with the throat while in *saṁhitā pāṭha* the connection is with the heart centre. Therefore, *saṁhitā pāṭha* creates the potential for the maximum energy to arise, like a string of gemstones, unified by a current of continuous energy but manifest as a series of discrete, perceptible, meaningful sound particles.

Anusvāra is the next level. It is a nasal sound made through the nose only and is also external. It can be heard occurring naturally in such words as *mantra* and *tantra*. It literally means 'after-sound' and occurs in spoken Sanskrit and recitation when a word ending in '*m*' is followed by a word beginning with a consonant. It causes the vowel which precedes the '*m*' to be nasal. It is as if the nasalization blends in a particular way and becomes immersed in the preceding vowel. This quality can be heard in such words as *saṁskrita* A further refinement is that the particular quality of the nasalization depends upon which of the five sets of letters in the Sanskrit alphabet the following sound belongs. In written form it is represented by a dot or *bindu* above the final letter of the first word.

There is an internal version of *anusvāra* used in Vedic recitation. This occurs when the syllable '*ghum*' replaces a nasalized '*ṁ*' sound. Two forms of *ghum* are mentioned in the *Yājñavalkya Śikṣā*, carrying different time measures and weight. They may be found in *saṁhitā pāṭha* but not in other forms of recitation as explained in the section on *vikṛtis* in Chapter 6. *Ghum* occurs, therefore, when the rules of *sandhi* are applied and it is interesting to notice how this change affects the subtle energies of the body. The example given is that of '*si ṭhaṁ hi asi*' when it occurs in *pada pāṭha*. But when it appears in *saṁhitā pāṭha* it has changed to '*si ghum hyasi*'. In the first version there is a nasal '*ṁ*' followed by a throat-resonating sound but in the second version a nasal *ghum* is followed by a heart-resonating sound.[32]

Anunāsika is a nasal sound made through both the nose and the mouth.[33] This is the second level and is again an external nasalization. It applies to the fifth letters of each of the five classes of mutes as well as to consonants and vowels.[34] In the north of India it may be referred to as '*candrabindu*' and is represented by a dot (*bindu*) within an upturned half-moon. Although it is associated with outward manifestations of sound it should at the same time bring about an internal resonance for, it is said, 'the nasal colour should arise from the heart, with a sound like that of bells'.[35]

Before Sanskrit became formalized as 'classical Sanskrit' *anunāsika* had further refinements.[36] This was part of the subtlety and precision of an older form of the language. The term *raṅga* is one example which is elaborated upon in some detail in the *Yājñavalkya Śikṣā*. It has a very particular and specific vibration or sound energy which affects the subtle body. The third chapter of the *Yājñavalkya Śikṣā* explains this in some detail. One example given is the word '*sadundubhe*'.[37] The nasalized sound on the '*n*', it says, should be made with the lips protruding in order to cause a central point of vibration so that it brings about a particular intensification of vibration.[38] A *raṅga* sound is one which may have the ringing quality of white copper temple gongs, or it may resemble the bright red *japā* flower whose pale centre is like the vowel while its outer, deeper, red colour represents the *raṅga anunāsika* vibration. It is described as resembling water which, having no colour of its own, can take on a colour if a dye is added to it. Similarly, a nasalization can take on the colour of the preceding vowel.[39] In music too a tone takes on the colour of a preceding tone. There may be occasions when, due to the laws of grammar, the nasalized '*n*' following the vowel disappears altogether. But does it? This *śikṣā* says that a touch of vibration remains like a shadow, just as when a rose petal which has rested in the palm of the hand is removed, the scent remains! These refined vibrations are designed to have a very subtle effect on the senses for those who can experience them, elevating the energies from gross to fine.

There are various other technical instructions given in this *śikṣā* about nasalization. The difference between them is often extremely fine, but if the intention is to affect the subtle body, which is of a much finer substance than the gross physical body, it is not surprising that such delicate distinctions have to be made. The poetic imagery used in the *Yājñavalkya Śikṣā* to describe these sound phenomena often gives an exquisite emotional touch to the dry technicalities of grammar. One might say that science and poetry unite in these descriptions, blending a keen eye for scientific observation with the emotional imagery of poetry.

Sometimes the term *anusvāra* is understood to include both *anunāsika* sounds and a group of nasal sounds referred to as *yama*. This third level of nasalization is an internal level for there may be no outward sound at all.[40] Attention to such subtle vibrations has disappeared from usage in the Sanskrit language.[41] The *yamas* ('twins' in this context) are nasal phonemes. They have no written forms but can be discerned by those familiar with this aspect of the language. They are produced at the root of the nose.

The beautiful refinement of this group of 'sounds' has to be experienced, but a *yama* can be described as a transitional sound intervening between a consonant and a nasal such as ordinarily occurs in words like '*padma*' where a slight hiatus occurs between 'd' and 'm' such that the oral stop after '*d*' and its nasal release on 'm' could be seen as a division of the '*d*' into two parts (twins) and written as '*paddma*'[42] The word '*svappna*' is a similar example. The first stage is an implosive stage of a sound which is not nasal. In the second stage air is pushed into the nasal cavity just before the following nasal sound is being formed. In this way the first sound, the non-nasal sound, becomes nasalized.[43] In *mantra* recitation any of the five groups of consonant sounds may become nasalized in a very subtle way and here the word *yama* refers to the doubling of non-nasal consonants; it is the second of the doubled consonants which is *yama*. In actual practice, it is the first letter which is uttered while it is the *dhvani* or *śruti* of the same duration as the repeated letter which occurs in the hiatus created by the doubling. Another way of describing what takes place can be appreciated if one takes an example from the group of guttural sounds. Between '*gh*' and the nasal of that group there is no outward sound, the 'sound' which exists is only a vibration in *madhyamā* (the subtle level of sound). This is for the purpose of *mantra* and is not in classical Sanskrit. It has been suggested, therefore, that *yama* is a form of embellishment of the Vedic language in recitation, designed to heighten the level of consciousness. These linguistic refinements found in *mantra* recitation preceded the development of some of the tonal movements (*gamakas*) which were subsequently used in music. They also indicate the true purpose of some of them, distinguishing them from other kinds of tonal movement which serve the purpose of 'surface decoration'.

Gaps

There can be doubling of consonants which is not associated specifically with nasalization. This is a technique which is used to create a particular sound effect. For example, when '*t*' is doubled the two sounds are pronounced as one but the first is 'kept in the mouth' while the other can be heard clearly outside.[44] The sensation of the '*t*' pronounced in this way, is felt within; an internal sound is experienced which affects the nervous system and the subtle body. The written text of the *Puruṣa Sūkta* (Hymn of Man) as recited by the Mādhyandina Branch of the *Śukla Yajurveda* shows plenty of evidence for the doubling of consonants, such rules for recitation being embedded in tradition.

It may be that the hiatus or 'gap' between the ending of a consonant and the beginning of a vowel is of ultimate significance. This is the 'gap' which can lead to perception of *nāda brahman*, perceivable in the four stages of *parā*, *paśyantī*, *madhyamā* and *vaikharī*.[45] Those who study the texts of the Vedas may comment on the syllables and how they combine sequentially to make words, phrases, verses and finally complete hymns. The aspect which is usually ignored is that behind all these units of sound, however small, there are gaps, and it is in these gaps, the apparent voids which are nothing of the sort, that the mechanics of transformation takes place. The principle is the same whether the gaps are between cells in the body or between minute sound elements. It has been argued that it is the organization of gaps within the Sanskrit language which gives rise to a language of such immense potential.

The gaps within the realm of music are equally significant. If Indian music does consist of 'innumerable small particles which coalesce' one could ask what actually takes place during the continuous transitions from particle to particle, from tone to tone, from *svara* to *svara*? Scientists may perceive this problem as one of quantifying time. In the transition from one speech sound to another or from tone to tone this interesting question will arise. The concept of the 'gap' has been expanded in Indian music both in a vertical as well as a horizontal sense. Copious use of different *gamakas* in Indian music, meaning in this instance any kind of movement between tones, reflects a process similar to vowel-consonant-vowel transition in speech.[46] Exploration of these transitional elements, or any vibrational phenomena, eventually leads to the realization that there is a non-temporal component which cannot be measured. This, in a manner of speaking, is the vertical component, the transcendental aspect.

Scientists and others have tried to express the same idea in their own language rather than the language of tradition. For example, if an open vowel sound such as '*a*' is followed by a completely closed consonant sound such as '*k*' or '*g*', there occurs a transition from an open sound to a point of contraction where there is no resonance at all. The language of quantum physics describes this as one sound collapsing onto another; the gap or hiatus which occurs at this point, before the resonance of the next vowel comes into existence, is one of silence, and in silence there exists intelligence. There is, therefore, a constant process of movement and rest, contraction and expansion. From the gap emerges the next sound. It has been suggested that this process of expansion and contraction of one sound onto another is the way in which impulses are transmitted through specific points of the nervous system. The impulses are conveyed from one neuron to another through the synaptic gaps which separate them. Gaps, it should be explained, occur naturally in creation; for example, at the physical level there is an interval between inhalation and exhalation and at the mental level between one activity and another, between one thought and another. They can be observed and, through practice, expanded.

There is another phenomenon which is not the same as a gap but which occurs when manifesting energy has come to a point of rest or standstill. This pause is called *viśrānti* meaning reposed, rested or ceased from, abated, coming to rest. Such a rest in consciousness is bliss (*ānanda*) and light (*prakāśa*).[47] The expression *viśrānti* is also used in the field of musical sound. Despite an emphasis on a flowing continuity of sound in Indian classical vocal music, which makes Western music seem permanently staccato to Indian musicians exposed only to their own culture, there must necessarily be pauses:

> ... *viśrānti* (coming to rest) is not only desirable, but necessary. The *nāda* [sound] we produce just cannot be continuous. Pauses or moments of silence are inevitable. *Viśrānti* is the requirement that such pauses should occur at the right place. No aspect of music is to appear rudely cut short. I have of course to end; but the pause must either appear as the gentle stilling of a flow, or as the climax of a passage.[48]

The momentary silence which immediately precedes the first articulated sound of a musical performance can transform a musical rendition, giving rise to a quite different aesthetic.

> There is a world of different between a *svara* that is merely thrust, abruptly and full-blown, into listening and one that is quietly breathed into silence, and made to crystallize gradually.[49]

Perhaps, after all, it is not the words or the notes on which we depend for our understanding but on the spaces between them. Would the words or notes make any sense without the 'gaps'? The discussion can be extended further depending on which level of temporal experience we are referring to. Indian music makes great use of this understanding for it is not always the number of notes that is important, especially in the unaccompanied slow *ālāpa* section. Often the important thing is how small an interval is of direct use and interest. This, of course, is the realm of *gamaka* (transitional tonal movement) and ornaments which is the subject of Chapter 7. The myriad types of tonal movements between substantive tones which can be heard in different styles of Indian music are not merely the mechanics of a particular style.

It is within the transitive elements of the music that the emotional and aesthetic potential lies.

Notes

1 Khan, *Music*, p. 57.

2 *Taittirīya Upaniṣad*, I.iii.2-4, trans. Swāmī Gambhirānanda.

3 *Kena Upaniṣad*, trans. Gambhirānanda, with commentary by Śankarācārya on Śloka 5.

4 Monier-Williams (1899), p. 300.

5 The Study Society, 'Record of Audiences with Śantānanda Saraswatī, Śankarācārya of Jyotir Maṭh in Northern India from 1953-1980', 1975, p. 57.

6 Record of Audiences with Śantānanda Saraswatī, The Study Society, London.

7 S. McIntosh, 'Sanskrit', *The Bridge*, no. 14, pp. 114-117.

8 Hans Jenny (1974), *Cymatics. Wave Phenomena, Vibrational Effects, Harmonic Oscillations with their Structure, Kinetics, and Dynamics*. Basilius Presse, Basel, Switzerland, vol. 2.

9 *Yājñavalkya Śikṣā*, 5:104.

10 *Yājñavalkya Śikṣā*, 1:35.

11 Swāmi Chetananda, 'The Symphony of Life', in Don Campbell, ed. *Music Physician for Times to Come*, Don Campbell, Quest Books, Theosophical Publishing House 1991, p. 293. 'Holography is a method of lensless photography in which the wave field of light scattered by an object is recorded on a plate as an interference pattern. When the photographic record – the hologram – is placed in

a coherent light beam like a laser, the original wave pattern is regenerated and a three-dimensional image appears. In fact, *any piece of the hologram will reconstruct the entire image*. Such are the manifest laws of nature.'

12 *Yājñavalkya Śikṣā*, 5:103.

13 D.S. Shannatoff-Khalsa and Yogi Bhajan (1989), *Sound Current Therapy and Self-Healing: The Ancient Science of Nād and Mantra Yoga* The Khalsa Foundation for Medical Science, Del Mar, CA, pp. 183-192.

14 *Aṣṭādhyāyī* of Pāṇini 1.1.9 Pāṇini's grammar describes the different kinds of articulation in detail, both inner and outer. Inner articulation is of five types, which are distinguished as formed by contact (*sparśāḥ*), slight contact (*īṣad spṛṣṭam* the semi-vowels) by being slightly open (*īṣad vivṛtam*), open (*vivṛtam*) and closed (*saṃvṛtam*). Outer articulation is of eleven types: open (*vivāra*), closed (*saṃvāra*), with breath (*śvāsa*), resonant (*nāda*), voiced (*ghoṣāḥ*), unvoiced (*aghoṣāḥ*), unaspirated (*alpaprāṇāḥ*), aspirated (*mahāprāṇāḥ*), raised accent (*udātta*), lowered accent (*anudātta*) and intermediary accent (*svarita*). See James Ballantyne (1995 ed.) *The Laghukaumudī*, A Sanskrit Grammar by Varadarāja, Motilal Banarsidass Pvt Ltd. Delhi, p. 6-7.

15 Shannatoff-Khalsa and Bhajan, 'functions of the hypothalamus such as (1) regulation of the autonomic nervous system (2) integration of reflexes and emotional reactions (3) activation and satisfaction of appetite (4) regulation of body temperature and (5) facilitation of brain impulses related to reflexive and skilled movement', pp. 183-186.

16 '*Maitri Upaniṣad*', 6.21 in Hume, p. 437.

17 Pūjyaśrī Chandraśekharendra Sarasvatī Svāmī (1995), *Hindu Dharma, The Universal Way of Life*, Bharatiya Vidya Bhavan, Bombay, p. 85.

18 H. Blavatsky, *Secret Doctrine*, vol. 2 p. 198.

19 Swami Rama, *Living with the Himalayan Masters*. Here it is said that the language of the Vedas is called *Nirukta*. The language of '*sandhya bhasha*', as it is referred to in this book, is completely based on sounds and the tones which can be made from those sounds are called 'the language of devas [gods]'. p. 8.

20 Sanskrit may be the root of the greatest number of languages in the world including the main languages of Europe, North India, Iran and the Middle East, but in these forms it does not have the same potential for the inner world as the original language does.

21 V.H. Deshpande (1973), *Indian Musical Traditions – An Aesthetic Study of the Gharanas in Hindustani Music*, Popular Prakashan, Bombay.

22 Raghava R. Menon, (1999), 'Dhvani, Nature and Culture of Sound', *Proceedings of International Seminar on Sound 1994*, Indira Gandhi National Centre for the Arts, New Delhi, pp. 55-63.

23 *Ṛg Veda*, 10.71.4.

24 Monier-Williams (1899), p. 861.

25 Patañjali, *Mahābhāṣya*, 1.2.40.

26 Nāradīya *Śikṣā* 1.7.9. Here pitch concepts are described: *dīpta* (shining, illuminated), *āyatā* (extended), *karuṇā* (mournful), *mṛdu* (soft or lowered), and *madhyamā* (moderate).

27 Mataṅga, 1.27-42

28 Monier-Williams (1899), p. 861.

29 Sharma, and Shringy, vol. 1, 24c-25b.

30 The dental sounds are *t, th, d, dh, n, l, s*. The palatal sounds are *c, ch, j, jh, ñ, y, ś*. See further Appendix 2.

31 The word *sandhi* is originally *sam*, a prefix meaning 'together' and *dhi* from the root *dhā* meaning 'to hold' – an example in itself of *sandhi*. When the '*m*' sound meets the '*dh*' sound it becomes an *anusvāra* and is pronounced as the nasal consonant of the same family to which the '*dh*' belongs, that is, the dental family. See Appendix 2.

32 *Yājñavalkya Śikṣā*, 2:58.

33 *Aṣṭādhyāyī* of Pāṇini, 1.1.8.

34 See Sanskrit alphabet – Appendix 2.

35 Sidney. W. Allen (1953), *Phonetics in Ancient India*, Oxford University Press, London, p. 40

36 Mishra, p. 71, and *Yājñavalkya Śikṣā*, 3:78.

37 *Yājñavalkya Śikṣā*, 3:64.

38 These instructions in the *Śikṣā* originate in those branches of ancient literature which contain *sūtras* from Lord Śiva (*āgamic śāstra*). They are part of the *śruti* collection.

39 *Yājñavalkya Śikṣā* 3:74-76.

40 These sounds exist in *madhyamā* and not in *vaikharī*. See in Chapter 1 'The Ear of the Heart – Levels of Sound'. *Anusvāra* and *bindu* are inseparable but while the former is pronounced in *vaikharī* and *madhyamā*, *bindu* relates only to *paśyantī* and *parā*.

41 Pāṇini's grammar gives only four specific instances of *yama* showing that the language to which this more extensive explanation of nasalization belongs is an older language, a language which was and still is used for the purposes of recitation.

42 Mishra, p.171.

43 *Yājñavalkya Śikṣā*, 5:91-95.

44 *Yājñavalkya Śikṣā*, 2:34.

45 See 'The Ear of the Heart – Levels of Sound' in Chapter 1.

46 Chaitanya B. Deva (1963), 'Transitive Elements in Music', *Nāda Rupa*.

47 Padoux, p. 257.

48 S.K. Saxena (1981), 'Aesthetics of Hindustani Music' in *Aesthetical Essays*, Chanakya Publications, Delhi, p. 162

49 Saxena, p. 162.

Chapter 3
Vedic Accents

What we call music in our everyday language is only a miniature, which our intelligence has grasped from that music or harmony of the whole universe which is working behind everything, and which is the source and origin of nature.[1]

Expression through music has to start somewhere. Perhaps it began with the most fundamental attribute of the human being, the voice. It has often been maintained that the origins of music are closely connected with language, with speaking. It may be that the natural state of spoken languages earlier on was closer to singing than to speech as we hear it today, that the human voice naturally communicated in a more musical way than is generally heard now. The subject of accents in Sanskrit, and particularly in Vedic Sanskrit, belongs to an oral culture when the sounded form was paramount. Undoubtedly the most sophisticated instrument for producing music is the human voice. It can also be said that everybody makes use of this musical instrument, that everybody sings whether they realize it or not; they do so when they speak. One has only to listen to the sound of different languages, where none of the meaning is understood, to discover that there are markedly different intonations, some languages sounding much more 'musical' than others. Indeed, it has been shown clearly that languages have different ranges of frequencies.[2]

Experience tells us that reciting together or singing together creates an energy which contributes towards a sense of well-being and harmony. It is unlikely that something so fundamental is a recent practice. One of the oldest known forms of singing together was the recitation of the Vedas. The hymns of the Vedas are formulae expressing eternal laws of creation. They are also songs of praise. As an ancient form of music, they showed how a certain use of tone and rhythm could bring about an energy which not only changed the quality and the capacity in an individual but also benefited the world. This form of recitation showed that there was a certain way of using time and rhythm, not always heard with the ears but nevertheless experienced by the subtle body, which brought about a greater equilibrium and harmony. It came to be known as the science of *mantra* or Mantra Yoga. Chanting the hymns of the Vedas or reciting the mantric formulae was an essential accompaniment to the Vedic sacrifices.

Essential to the practice of Vedic ritual was the Vedic fire altar. These altars were built to a specific formula; the design was based on numbers which relate to the difference between the solar and lunar year,[3] a discrepancy based on the same cosmic principle which we find reflected in the 'comma of Pythagoras' and in the ancient system of *grāmas*.[4] Moreover, the organization of the material of the *Ṛg Veda*, the oldest of the four Vedas handed down to the present day, is reflected in the formula for the design of altars.[5] Knowledge such as this is surely impressive as it must reflect the results of acute observation over a considerable period of time. A source of chronological evidence for this can be found in references in the *Purāṇas* (encyclopaedias of ancient knowledge) which date back as far as the fourth millennium BC and may be earlier than that. Such evidence strongly suggests a mature scientific knowledge which preceded that of the Greeks. If one accepts this evidence, the implications for the existence of a musical culture of an equivalent maturity, in terms of scientific understanding if not in aesthetic development, are also strong.

It is often maintained that the way the Vedic hymns have been chanted represents the beginnings of Indian music as we currently hear it. Consequently, much investigation and discussion has taken place as to the possible connection between them and an emerging musical system, the supposition being that there was a sequential evolution. But is this supposition correct? When other aspects of musical evolution in India are taken into account, the development is much more likely to have been a process of many layers coming together, a variety of strands of influence interweaving at different times.

The system of sound organization for different traditions of Vedic recitation (but not including *Sāma Veda* recitation), which has been handed down through the oral tradition to the present day, involved the use of up to three accents. At first the *Ṛg Vedic* hymns, it is said, were sung on one note, in a monotone and without melodic life. This hymnal period has been called *ārchika*.[6] Another early period of Vedic recitation pivoted around two notes, referred to as *udātta* and *anudātta*. They are also referred to as *brāhmaṇa svaras* and described as belonging to the *gātha* or *gātika* period. In the course of time a third intermediary tone known as *svarita,* was established. This period of Vedic music is known as *sāmika.*

What were the three accents? A variety of descriptions exist. Moreover, the situation increases in complexity as colour, deity, caste, seer and metre are attributed to each accent, as the opening verses of the *Yājñavalkya Śikṣā* describe. For it is the way in which the tones are arranged in a *mantra* which gives rise to a particular energy within every sentence, an understanding which is only available to those familiar with the correlation of sounds, colours and hierarchies in the Cosmos. Moreover the *vikṛtis*, referred to in Chapter 6, which are methods of division and repetition of the words of a hymn, alter the energy pattern of the original form (*saṁhitā pāṭhaḥ*). Each modification introduces a different energy. After such modifications, recitation of the verse in its first form reinstates the original pattern of energy. The Vedas, unlike the Upaniṣads which are a refinement of the Vedic teaching, deal with the mechanics of the many levels of existence, and with man's connection and resonance with beings and energies in this hierarchy.

The relationship of the accents to the text is a subject beyond the scope of this book but a frequently quoted image conveys clearly the underlying principle. As the *Yājñavalkya Śikṣā* describes, the sequence of sounds in *mantra* recitation is like a necklace or garland (*mālā*). It is the resonance of the vowels which constitutes the thread, while the beads represent the consonants which have no resonance of their own but take on those of the vowels and, like a necklace, follow the shape given by the positions of the vowels.

How were these accents full of such potential to be produced? The exact nature and origin of the accents has given rise to considerable speculation. The grammarian Pāṇini refers to *udātta* as 'high', *anudātta* as 'low', and *svarita* as 'a compound tone'.[7] It should be understood from this reference that these accents refer to the outer articulation of vowels and not necessarily to pitch; they relate to positions in the mouth. The same grammarian explains that *svarita* is the combination of two accents or tones, *udātta* being the first and *anudātta* the second.[8]

Elsewhere *udātta* may be referred to as 'raised' and *anudātta* as 'not raised'. It would seem that in the course of time the accents became musical tones, referred to as *svaras*, for it is said that both *udātta* and *anudātta* can be distinguished as discrete pitch entities while *svarita* is a combination of the other two. A number of scholars have deduced that not only was there a connection between accent and musical pitch but that there is also a correspondence with the Greek acute, grave and circumflex accents.

> The Vedic like the ancient Greek accent, was a musical one, depending mainly on pitch, as is indicated both by its not affecting the rhythm of metre, and by the name of the chief tone, *udātta*, 'raised'. That such was its nature is, moreover, shown by the account given of it by the ancient nature phoneticians.[9]

It is perhaps not surprising that this association has arisen for the term *svara*, in Indian terminology, is a flexible one. It can mean a vowel, a syllable or a tone depending on the context in which it is used.[10]

However, we disagree with the statement made by Fox Strangways that: 'The *Ṛg Veda* is recited now, as it has always been, to three tones, for the accent was originally a mark of musical pitch'.[11] Not only do the accents seem to originate in the domain of language, but with so little historical information to draw on it is not possible to say categorically that practice has been consistently the same. We know from present-day practice that the *Brāhmanas* and parts of the *Ṛg Veda* are recited using only two accents. The *Dhātu Pāṭhaḥ*, already referred to in Chapter 1, has been traditionally chanted using three accents. There is nothing to show what the musical relationship of the accents was in any context in which they were used, though it is presumed that the pitches were relative rather than absolute.

If we accept that the accents were linguistic in origin, it would seem that they acquired tonal qualities over a period of time and were further enhanced as a reference in *Nāradīya Śikṣā*, which pertains to recitation of the *Ṛg Veda*, says:

It should be known that there is *dīptā* in the *udātta* and it is known that *dīptā* is there in the *svarita*. *Mṛdu* is known to be in the *anudātta*. This is the excellence of the *śrutis* in the Gandharva (music).[12]

Dīptā implies 'brightness' and as such qualifies both the 'raised' tone and the 'compound' or connecting tone. *Mṛdu* suggests a quality of relative 'softness' which thus characterizes the 'lowered' tone. These descriptions may, of course, be qualifying the three accents, but they may also reflect a later development as subtlety of sound perception developed. If the latter explanation is accepted, it shows early signs of a sound system which was to develop and be described in considerable minutiae of detail in subsequent musicological treatises.

The qualities and characteristics of *svarita* as a 'compound tone' should be addressed in particular, as the use of this tone is not as straightforward as the other two accents and there are special reasons why this is so. It is beyond the remit of this book to discuss all the various forms which this accent can take, but some indication of its complexity will be given.

In general, this 'sounded' tone, the *svarita*, occurs between the two others in pitch. It is formed according to the rules of *sandhi* (junction), by the most euphonious combination of two primary vowels already bearing separate musical accents. (*Sandhi* can also be implied in the etymology of a word as well as being applied when two words coalesce.) Depending on the way in which it is pronounced each vowel has a particular vibration; a number of formants may be detected for each vowel giving each a characteristic frequency. This means that the *svarita* accent when it arises – for example in the *Ṛg Veda* – out of the fusion of two vowels, as a result of the application of the rules of *sandhi*, possesses a particular vibration.

However, there is divergence of views about the exact nature of this tone and its practice. Traditions vary. Some say that it begins at the level of the raised tone (*udātta*) and the rest is at the level of the lowered tone (*anudātta*), others that it is a continuous fall (*pravaṇa*) – or does this mean glide if the term *pravaṇa* is taken to mean 'downhill slope'?[13] Similarly, *svarita* is described as a combination of two accents: the first half is the raised tone and the latter part is 'made to fall' (*praṇihanyate*);[14] or it may be described as 'cast down' or 'shaken'. That authoritative treatise on the *Ṛg Veda*, the *Ṛk Prātiśākya*, is more specific, giving time values, saying that the first half of the *mātra* (measure of time) of the *svarita* is higher than the raised tone while the rest is *anudātta*. From these descriptions we may try to reconstruct in our minds what *svarita* sounds like.

It is also said that the Vedic *svarita* arises out of the low accent when it is preceded by the high accent. This means that the low accent starts higher than the preceding high accent, making it like an ornamented *udātta*. It is likely that the *svarita* accent arising as a result of natural fluctuations above and below the basic sound, acquired certain characteristics through usage.

Uttered alone it is an independent sound but in chant it becomes a glide. This glide is associated with a descending movement from the tone above to the tone below, a characteristic in keeping with the general tendency for archaic music to use descending melodic forms. The exertion required for the voice to move in this way during recitation means that it may acquire, in the first part of the sound, a touch of a pitch which is higher than the 'tone above'. Thus the pitch of the original accent, plus a movement above the raised tone, together with its gliding descent, constitute *svarita*. In this way *svarita* is an accent which has the sense of 'graced'[15] and, as such, may have heralded the extensive use of tonal movement (*gamaka*) which is so characteristic of subsequent styles of Indian music.

It is not surprising that an exact definition of *svarita* is elusive for it consists of various types. One detailed source of information describes eight different varieties of *svarita*.[16] A particular distinction is that of dependent and independent *svaritas*.[17] The first form is explained as a joining together of a 'raised' and 'lowered' accent and this is a very usual form of *svarita* accent, while the independent form is a substitute for a 'lowered' tone when it follows a 'raised' tone. This latter form may have arisen from the blending (*sandhi*) of two syllables one of which was an *udātta*. The relationship between these two types of *svarita* is close, but as far as the ear is concerned, the differentiation takes place at the level of nuance, a level of subtlety of sound awareness to which, generally speaking, we no longer pay attention. If one of the purposes of *mantra* recitation is to raise the level of energy or consciousness in order to realize *adṛṣta phalla*, the unseen fruit or result, it is not surprising to discover that linguistic sound techniques have become woven into the fabric of recitation to achieve this purpose.

In general the *svarita* accent can be described as a moving tone, but it is the interplay of the three accents or tones which is crucial to its effect. Texts such as the *Yājñavalkya Śikṣā* explain the rules which govern their arrangement. If *svarita* is a transitional tone between a raised tone and a lowered tone, one would expect it to occur only after a raised tone and not after a lowered tone. But this is not always the case. It is quite usual for two or more raised tones to appear consecutively in a Vedic sentence. When this occurs the second of the raised tones is followed by a lowered tone, not a *svarita*, if the lowered tone is then followed by a raised tone. Although the final raised tone (*udātta*) of this sequence is a fixed accent which cannot be changed, it can, however, disappear. When this happens the lowered tone will be followed by a *svarita*. This *svarita* is 'independent' of the *udātta*, which has disappeared. The formula looks as follows: a situation which is actually U + U + A + U becomes U + U + A + S, showing a *svarita* following an *anudātta* accent.

Another characteristic associated with *svarita* is that of *pracaya* ('multitude'). The rule says that if a low accent follows a *svarita* then it is called *pracaya*. Those who know the essence of the Vedas, those great thinkers of the Vedas, know this *anudātta* as *pracaya* or *ekasvara*.[18] *Pracaya* is the joining of *anudātta* and *udātta* taking 50 per cent in time-value from each accent, elsewhere referred to as a 'dependent' *svarita*. As far as the textual tradition is concerned, this accent is not shown by the conventional mark for a *svarita* accent, but it *is* indicated in a much earlier form of unwritten notation, the manual gestures or *mudrās*. This is an interesting feature which the *Yājñavalkya Śikṣā* describes, saying that, if a *mantra* ends with a *svarita*, the hand indicates this by moving smoothly without a jerk. If a *svarita* is followed by a *pracaya*, then this will be indicated by a jerk of the hand in a downward direction.[19]

However ancient the system of three accents, it is nevertheless likely to have been an advance on something simpler. Three notes are already more 'musical' to the ear than a single note, though reciting using only a single note emphasizes the rhythmic element (*chandas*) as only by manipulating this dimension can any variation be introduced. Verses (*ṛks*) can also be recited using only two tones which then introduces another dimension of change. Thus all can be seen to be a progression. There is a particular intensity about the prolonged repetition of three notes when they are closely related in pitch. Any variation, however small, creates a major impression. While one element of variation is the rhythmic component of the *mantras*, another is brought about by specific subtleties of pronunciation. These three components combine to create a system of considerable potential. Recitation of the *Ṛg Veda* and *Yajur Veda* in this way represents a very particular discipline.

In *Sāma Veda* recitation, when more than three tones are used to chant portions of the Veda, the sound is no longer bound to this fixed threefold shape. We could say that the fixed form, like frozen ice, has melted, allowing a degree of greater tonal fluidity. This is one school of thought, but there could equally have been two independent systems.

An area of great interest, particularly in connection with the evolution of musical systems, is the relationship between the three tones of recitation and the seven tones of other forms of music. Speculation abounds as to how this connection works. We start the discussion with a popular notion that the three varieties of accent turned into the seven available tones of the chantings of the *sāmans* which later became handed down as the system of *sargama*, *sa*, *re*, *ga*, *m*, *pa*, *dha*, *ni*, *sa*. If this idea is true then how did it come about?

There is, for example, a theory which arises from the subdivision of the three accents, viz. *udātta*, *udāttatara*, *anudātta*, *anudāttatara*, *svarita*, *svaritodatta* and *ekaśruti*. Initially these distinctions related to the position of the sound in the mouth and the particular effort required to make the sound. *Anudāttatara* refers to the lowest sound, one which immediately precedes an *udātta* or raised tone, and *ekaśruti* indicates a tone without accent. While, no doubt, this expansion of the threefold idea represents a natural morphological process, it is not entirely clear whether these additional accents were ever discrete pitches or whether they originated as intonations to enhance meaning and later became specific pitches. The question is particularly relevant to the rendition of *Sāma Veda*. As the commentary on the *Nāradīya Śikṣā* points out: 'The number of the *Ṛg Veda svaras* varies from seven to three according to different works. Thus Patañjali believes that there were seven *svaras*, which he refers to as *udātta*, *udattatara*, *anudātta*, *anudāttatara*, *svarita*, *udātta* forming a part of *svarita*, differing from the other *udātta*.'[20] The question we are left with is whether this is an attempt to define and expand an existing sound system which later became understood as music in terms of a scale of notes, or whether these 'intonations' were forerunners of a variety of forms of tonal movement (*gamaka*) which were later described in such detail by writers of musical treatises (the *śāstras*)?

For the different schools of Vedic recitation there were reference manuals for detailed examination of phonetic questions (*prātiśākhyas*). In addition there were a plethora of phonetic manuals known as *śikṣās*. The oldest of these may predate the *prātiśākhyas* but in general it is accepted that, if there is variance between the *śikṣās* and the *prātiśākhyas*, the latter takes precedence. For example, the *prātiśākhyas* often differ from Pāṇini. A work known as the *Pariśikṣā* explains that the first note '*ṣaḍja*' (*Sa*) and the second note '*ṛsabha*' (*Re*) arise from the low accent (*anudātta*); the third note '*gāndhāra*' (*Ga*) and the fourth '*madhyama*' (*Ma*) from the high accent (*udātta*); and the fifth, sixth and seventh notes, *pañcama* (*Pa*), *dhaivata* (*Dha*) and *niṣāda* (*Ni*) come from the *svarita* accent. The seventh note in particular is said to arise from the *abhinihita* and *kṣaipra* varieties of *svarita* while the sixth note is said to be produced from two different versions (*tairovyañjna* and *pratihata*) of the 'compound tone'. How this complex theoretical explanation relates to practice needs to be demonstrated by someone with direct experience otherwise the authority of this source of information is questionable.[21]

The *Nāradīya Śikṣā* also states that the seven notes of the musical scale originate from the three accents, but this *śikṣā* differs from the previous description about the relationship between the accents and the notes. The *Yājñavalkya Śikṣā* reiterates the *Nāradīya Śikṣā*. The question is whether these theories represent direct experience and an elevated level of acoustical perception or whether they are speculative ways of relating the phenomena of three to that of seven. In practice, musicians may describe the relationship of three tones to seven tones in a variety of different ways with some of these descriptions making use of relationships between fixed tones and the harmonic series to which they give rise. From these perceived relationships a series of seven tones spanning an octave can be derived.

One theory which does not relate tones to the harmonic series is as follows: if any three adjacent tones are selected, as may be found in *Ṛg Veda* and *Kṛṣṇa Yajur Veda* styles of recitation, and named *Ga*, *Ma*, *Re* – the third, fourth and second scale degrees – and a similar pattern of three tones are selected but at a different pitch, such as *Dha*, *Ni*, *Pa* – the sixth, seventh and fifth scale degrees – it can be seen that they virtually make up two tetrachords of a scale. Six tones with only one missing, the tonic (*Sa*), which would complete an octave. Interestingly, the *Dha*, *Ni*, *Pa* configuration is a feature of the descending *Sāma Veda* scale of tones. Another configuration which echoes Vedic recitation could be described in terms of the tonic, the seventh below and the third above the tonic *Sa*, *Ni*, *Sa*, *Ga*, *Sa*. Its approximate counterpart in the upper tetrachord would be the fifth, the fourth and the seventh – *Pa*, *Ma*, *Pa*, *Ni*, *Pa*. Thus, it is speculated, a scale of seven tones could have evolved from three tones through a system of tetrachords.

By this stage of speculation it would be reasonable to wonder whether the three accents described in the *Nāradīya Śikṣā* and the *Yājñavalkya Śikṣā* and the musical system of seven tones to which they are said to relate belong to the same period of history. As has been suggested before it is entirely possible that the tonal system used in *Sāma Veda* recitation had a different source from that of the system of accents used for *Ṛg Veda* and *Yajur Veda mantra* recitation. Among the different traditions of recitation which use accents there is interesting variation and it is worth noting in this connection the particular style of recitation used by vedins of the *Śukla* (White) *Yajur Veda*, Mādhyandina branch. This style differs significantly from that used in the *Kṛṣna* (Black) branch of *Yajur Veda* recitation and that used in the *Ṛg Veda* tradition. The *Śukla Yajur Veda* style of recitation makes use of three accents but it is the special system of hand signs (*mudrās*) accompanying the chant which is faithful to the language of the *mantra*.[22]

What is important is that the three accents, representing a 'Law of Three', especially when combined with the use of gestures (*mudrās),* can be seen as the basis of an important esoteric psychology for they not only represent a simple musical system but are a way of modulating energy and perception. This is explained in more detail in Chapter 4 on the gestures (*mudrās*) which accompany *Śukla* (White) *Yajur Veda* recitation, Mādhyandina branch. The accents can be said to represent an active, passive and mediating force *udātta*, *anudātta* and *svarita*, respectively, and, as such, represent three interacting energies.

Evidence suggests that both the method of accents and the system of seven tones represent musical systems based on knowledge which reflects the laws of the universe. Thus it can be said that two fundamental laws are represented. The initial manifestation of the universe or manifest world requires a combination of three forces, often referred to in *Sāṅkhya* philosophy as the three *guṇas*, but for its development and expansion it depends on the 'Law of Seven' which complements it by representing a repetitive sequence of events arising from the same initial origin. These two laws, arising directly from an ultimate, all pervasive Source, previously described in this book as *Om*, operate together throughout the universe at every level. In the human being the three forces can be said to represent the nervous system which acts as a channel for energy to animate life, a theory which accords directly with the teaching on the three pathways of energy and the commentary given on this in the *Yājñavalkya Śikṣā*. It can also be seen that the system of three tones deviates less from the Source, the One, than does the system of seven tones. It therefore represents, in potential, a more direct approach to a reconnection with this ultimate Source. The pervasiveness of seven, a number which is very familiar to human psychology in, for example, the form of the seven days of the week or the seven basic tones of the scale, represents a greater level of deviation from the Source. The question is how, in musical terms, can release be obtained from this bondage with time? In the Indian tradition of music, part of the answer lies in what takes place between the steps of the scale of seven tones. The preoccupation, therefore, which has taken place at different times in Indian musicological history, with trying to explain how three accents gave rise to a scale of seven notes can be understood as an expression of a fundamental concept.[23]

Notes

1 Khan, *Music*, p. 7.
2 Tomatis, p. 71.
3 Feuernstein, Kak and Frawley, pp. 201-206.
4 For *Grāmas*, see 'Tonal Sequences and Octave Species' in Chapter 5.
5 Feuerstein, Kak and Frawley (1999), *In Search of the Cradle of Civilization*, Motilal Banarsidass Publishers Pvt. Ltd. Delhi, p. 203.
6 G.H. Tarlekar (1995), *Sāman Chants: In Theory and Present Practice*, Sri Satguru Publications, Delhi, p. 21.
7 Pāṇini, *Aṣṭādhyāyī*, 1.2.29, 1.2.30, 1.2.31.
8 Pāṇini, *Aṣṭādhyāyī* 1.2.32. Also Mishra, p. 220.
9 Macdonell, p. 448.
10 See 'Words for Sound' in Chapter 1.
11 A.H. Fox Strangways (1994), *The Music of Hindostan*, Munshiram Manoharlal Pvt. Ltd., New Delhi, p. 246.
12 *Nāradīya Śikṣā* 1.7.18.
13 Sidney W. Allen (1953), *Phonetics in Ancient India*, Oxford University Press, London, p. 88.
14 Allen, pp. 87-88.
15 Strangways, p. 246.
16 The *śikṣā* which pertains to the *Śukla Yajurveda Prātiśākhya*, the *Yājñavalkya Śikṣā*, describes eight different varieties referred to as *jātya, abhinihata, kṣaipra, praśliṣṭa, tairovyañjana, tairovirāma, pādavṛtta, tathābhāvya*, (1:76-77).
17 For an illustrated example, see Allen pp. 88-9.
18 *Yājñavalkya Śikṣā*, 1:58-59.
19 *Yājñavalkya Śikṣā*, 1:89.
20 Paṭañjali, *Mahābhāṣya*, 1.2.33. Cited by Mishra V. (1972) p. 220.
21 Mishra, p. 221.
22 With the advent of a written form, a system of markings for accents evolved; conventionally an *udātta* accent has no marking, an *anudātta* accent is indicated by a horizontal line beneath the syllable and the *svarita* accent has a vertical line above the syllable. See Monier-Williams 'Sanskrit Grammar' for a preliminary introduction to the system of markings.
23 The relationship between these two laws is encapsulated in the universal symbol consisting of a circle of nine points, the enneagram, which shows how they combine. The question remains, in musical terms, as to how to escape from the confines of seven. This question invites discussion which is beyond the remit of this book. However, it intimates that consideration should be given to both the 12 *svara* positions within the octave as well as the system of 22 *śrutis* outlined in Chapter 5. Another aspect is mentioned in Chapter 7.

Chapter 4

The Hand – *Mudrās*

It is probable that the earliest attempts at notation were made by the Hindus and Chinese from whom the principle was transferred to Greece.[1]

But were they? At present the earliest known example of its kind, is the seventh-century Kuḍumiyāmalai rock inscription which consists of seven compositions, one in each of the seven original *grāma rāgas*; the notation is based upon the seven solmization syllables (*sargama*).[2] This system of solmization is still in use at the present time, Indian notation existing in a basic form of seven *sargama* (solfa) syllables, though interestingly an early idea of octave (*saptaka*) meant the seven intervals between tones.[3]

So far, it is understood that the earliest forms of writing anywhere in the world were cuneiform used by the Mesopotamians and hieroglyphics invented by the Egyptians about 5000 years ago. In India the system of transmission of knowledge was an oral one. Writing developed because the capacity for memory declined. The same situation existed for music; if there existed any graphic system of representing tone at that time, or indeed earlier, it has been lost long ago. However, there does exist something comparable but probably very much older, though it is not possible to say how old. These are the manual gestures prescribed to accompany certain branches of Vedic recitation, in particular, recitation of the *Sāma Veda* and the *Yajur Veda* which both make use of a system of hand movements (*mudrās*). The system of cheironomy used for the recitation of *Sāma Veda* is described in a variety of sources and we do not propose to repeat these descriptions here although, necessarily, some explanation may be required in order to further the discussion.[4] Description will, however, centre mainly on the recitation of *Yajur Veda* as described in the *Yājñavalkya Śikṣā*[5] and as explained to the writer by Dr H.R. Sharma.[6]

In the age which preceded the present one, which is Kali yuga, it is said that there were many Vedas. Śri Candraśekharendra Sarasvatī, once Śankarācarya of the South of India, explained how the sage Vyāsa classified some of the knowledge known as Veda into four parts; for he said:

> In the Yuga that is to commence, the life-span of people will be short; their memory-power will be weak; the supernormal powers of Yoga will decrease; something should be done in order to save the Veda from utter destruction.

We look back to a time when Vedic recitation and ritual took place within a cultural and social context which, as far as we know, existed when indigenous religions were strongly iconic,[7] when there was a predominance of goddess-worship and acknowledgement of the feminine principle among people. Until further research brings additional information to light, it has been suggested that this was the situation up until 5000 years ago. In the course of time things began to change so that around 3000 years ago the predominance of the goddess image had begun to disappear. It would appear that within this setting there seems to have existed a culture which was predominantly aural rather than visual, with an emphasis on the ear as an organ for receiving information from the external world. This 'aural' culture made use of a system of cheironomy or gesture during recitation. Exactly how this came about is not at all clear. We can say that the language of gesture must have started somewhere, that there must have been a time when symbolic thought required articulation in some way. The hands are the most basic instruments of non-verbal expressive communication and a refinement of this would be the use of the fingers, or first of all perhaps just one finger, as in pointing.

The language of gesture and neurophysiology are intimately connected. Contemporary scientific research may be undergoing a resurgence of interest in the relationship between sound and neurophysiology, but the situation is as old as mankind. It will be useful to the following discussion, therefore, to discuss briefly the different roles played by each hemisphere of the brain. It is not proposed to give a detailed explanation but some background information may help to appreciate the intelligence behind the design of this system of cheironomy, this very early form of sound notation. In talking about brain organization it will be assumed here that someone who is right-handed will be left-brain dominant as this is the situation for the majority of people.

A major right-brain feature is the ability to appreciate music. This holds true even when the left brain has been rendered useless as a result of stroke or other injury, as contemporary neurophysiological research has shown. The right brain is also primarily responsible for perceiving space and making judgements. It relates amongst other things to feeling associated states, images and music. Inflection and rhythm which belong in this domain are musical qualities and also crucial components of speech. It is within anyone's experience that particular enunciation and emphasis of words or phrases, the emotional quality, can radically alter the meaning or perception of what is being communicated. Pattern recognition is also a right-brain function, as is the capacity to decipher hand gestures. Speech, which is essentially a left-brain activity, is consequently enhanced by the use of gesture which has a right-brain appeal. It is also enhanced by the connecting of rhythm to speech.

Scientific experiment has shown that the left ear, which connects with the right hemisphere, can pick up emotion in a voice much better than the right ear and left hemisphere. So, it would seem that to change conscious states, right-hemisphere techniques are needed which means using rhythm and emotion in a particular way.

So what were the sound forms used by those reciting the Vedas when the kinaesthetic and aural phenomenon seemed to be a single concept? Does the efficacy of the knowledge contained in the *Yājñavalkya Śikṣā*, have a neurological basis? The *Yājñavalkya Śikṣā*, considered to be one of the three main *Śikṣās*, describes in detail, by means of a series of metrical couplets (*ślokas*), how recitation should take place.[8] The purpose of the account given in this chapter is to represent some of the information given in the *Yājñavalkya Śikṣā* as part of a larger picture which the book, as a whole, aims to present.

Yajur Veda Recitation

Yājña is the performance of ritual actions or oblations. The word itself is derived from the root '*yaj*' meaning 'to worship'. In Vedic sacrifice, *mantras* are recited in association with the meaning of the action or ritual which is being performed. These rituals have both an outward physical form as well as a counterpart at another level of refinement. When the *Yajur Veda* (Mādhyandina branch of *Śukla Yajur Veda*) is recited on its own, without ritual, the manual gestures (*mudrās*) accompany the recitation throughout. When the *mantras* are recited during the sacrifice there are no gestures because, by this stage, their meaning and energy has been internalized. This is an important aspect of tradition. These hand signs (*mudrās*) are associated, therefore, with the subtle form of the sacrifice while the physical outward form of the ritual takes place. The word *mudrā* is derived from the verbal root *mud* meaning 'to be happy', to give pleasure', 'to exhilarate'. It is interesting, from the point of view of the discussion which follows, that these interpretations give the sense of movements which are designed to raise the energy level and stimulate happiness.

Preparation

The first and very important stage of *mantra* recitation is preparation. The commentary on the relevant *śloka* explains that the student should be seated facing the teacher (*guru*), cross-legged, with a straight back and with both up-turned hands resting on his knees. In both the *Nāradīya Śikṣā* and the *Yājñavalkya Śikṣā* the relationship between the *guru* and the disciple is emphasized indicating that the *guru* system was well-established when the relevant sections of the *śikṣā* were put together.

The student should wait for the permission of the *guru* to start and should not think about other things. He (students are traditionally male) should keep his right elbow on the upper third part of the right thigh and place the fist of the left hand beneath the elbow (Figure 4.1).

Figure 4.1 Preparation for *mantra* recitation

At first it would seem that this instruction merely describes the most convenient way of supporting the right elbow and assisting ease of movement of the right arm. However, we would like to refer once more to the scientific information available with regard to the different functions of the hemispheres of the brain. Essentially the right side is emotional, spatial and non-verbal, whereas the left side is verbal, sequential and very much involved with language skills. Humans who are right-handed, and this is the majority, will avoid using the left hand for tasks requiring action and will tend to use the left hand for receptive, passive tasks such as cradling a baby. In general, the left hand holds or contains what the right hand takes. This situation is precisely represented in the instruction given to the intending student of recitation. We may also note that in this ancient system of oral transmission it was the hand that showed the *mudrās* that was later to become the hand that held the pen. However, there are other reasons for using the right hand, as we shall discuss. A process which contrasts with this takes place when, for example, a student learns Indian music in a traditional way. The requirement is that the student plays the *tānpurā* (the long-necked, lute-like drone instrument) using the right hand in a repetitive passive sense while it is the left hand which carries out the actions of expressive gesture and timekeeping. This is a left-hand/right-brain connection which no doubt alters brain pathways through repeated practice.

The *Śikṣā* continues. The student should be in a happy mood and leaning forward a little with his head and mouth lowered. (In other words, the chin should be lowered.) He should keep his eyes on the palm of the right hand (which is cupped like a cow's ear) for it is the right hand which evokes the Law of Three in the form of the three accents of recitation.[9] Therefore he should be mentally prepared, being in a state of attention with a focussed mind. The *dharma* or rule for these instructions, says the commentary, is based on a science given by the *ṛṣis* or seers.[10] Focussing the eyes in this way encourages the mind to become still and enables the upward movement of energy. The principle of eye focus in physical movement is an important one and can be found in spiritual traditions belonging to other cultures. As far as the Indian tradition is concerned, the idea is reinforced by the *Cārāyaṇīya Śikṣā.* This *Śikṣā* (phonetic manual) pertains to recitation of the *Ṛg Veda* and is specific on the relationship of hand to eye.

> One should always articulate the accent properly, indicating the direction of the accent by a movement of the hand. In the case of the high accent, one should cast a contracted glance of the right eye on the junction between the nose, the cheeks and the eyebrows.[11]

What is the relevance of this instruction? The hand has to connect with the right eye in order to generate the required subtle energy. This is a physical instruction which has its effect at the subtle level.[12] Just as the right ear has a different subtle capacity from the left ear (as has been previously described) similarly the right eye differs from the left. It is also true that at the physical level the functions of the two ears are not physiologically identical. If the question is asked as to why the right hand has to be used for these gestures (*mudrās*), then the answer emerges clearly that the hand has to connect with the right eye. Further reinforcement for this idea may be drawn from reference to the *Māṇḍūkya Upaniṣad* (verse 3) where the right eye is described as the doorway or place of experience of the external world in the physical (waking) state. The commentary which accompanies the verse explains that it is through the right eye that the soul perceives form.[13] Thus it can be appreciated that none of these instructions are working at the level of an aerobics workout but are beautifully designed to raise the individual's level of subtle energy.

Turning now to a contemporary scientific reference which stresses a different aspect of the hand-eye connection, we find that Dr Alfred Tomatis, an ear, nose and throat specialist, surgeon, psychologist and inventor in France, spent at least 50 years redefining the ear's special significance in relation to the voice. In connection with his treatment of dyslexia he made a discovery which is curiously pertinent to the instructions given in this ancient source of information, the *Yājñavalkya Śikṣā*:

> We advise the child when he leaves us to continue reading at home every day, in a loud, clear voice. I mentioned earlier the importance I attach to this exercise. It is not only those who suffer, or have suffered, from dyslexia who should do this, but the entire population, adults as well as children, those able to juggle with words as much as those who are intimidated by words. Reading aloud half an hour daily seems to me the minimum to be prescribed. Besides its deep though not always visible benefits, this method offers an advantage that may be immediately appreciated: *it ensures a most effective storage of information* [my italics]. I often repeat to my clients that what has been learned in this way is never forgotten ...
>
> A child who learns his lessons by repeating them aloud assimilates them – more slowly, yes, but also much more securely and lastingly. The benefit will be still greater

> if he takes care – and this is what we ask our young clients to do – *to speak towards the right hand and particularly the area of the skin between the thumb and the index finger* [my italics]. In this way, lateralization is strengthened, and this is always favourable to self-affirmation and self-realization.[14]

Tomatis does not explain in his book how he gained his knowledge of treatment for dyslexic children but this particular connection between the beliefs of the 'ancients', as they are often referred to, who relied totally on an oral tradition, and contemporary scientific thought is worth noting. The neurological intelligence which underlies this very old set of instructions should not be underestimated. Indeed, it is said that quite 50 per cent of our hearing process depends upon memory. If this is the case, then there are neurological implications for learning the spoken and musical language of another culture because retraining the memory may be as important as acquiring different mechanical skills.

The correct procedures for proper recitation having been established, one final piece of advice is given; the person who wants to recite the Vedas should keep his body in the same way that a tortoise does, his limbs withdrawn. In other words, his awareness of the world around him should be withdrawn to avoid distraction and help focus the attention.

When gestures are used while reciting the Vedic *mantras* during the sacrificial ritual they should be used correctly to show where the accents occur. One might ask why this is important. The reason given is that he who does not recite properly does not attain the fruits of the sacrifice. But what are the fruits of the sacrifice? The explanation given is that, just as we eat food which gives energy, so *mantras* recited without using accents are like food which fails to provide energy; something vital is missing.[15]

Again scientific observation enhances this statement in the *Yājñavalkya Śikṣā*. Dr Tomatis believed that the ear's primary function is to charge the neo-cortex of the brain and thereby the entire nervous system. To him, sound is a nutrient and when we are not able to assimilate the full spectrum of sound frequency, the ramifications parallel the inability to digest food. The essential difference is that, while food fuels the body, sound-waves, 'digested' by the ear, provide electrical impulses that charge the brain. He believed that there is an energizing effect in music and vocal sounds which are rich in certain frequencies. Gregorian chant was his music of choice to illustrate this observation. His work with Benedictine monks led him to discover that the act of chanting was what gave the monks so much energy, even though they slept little and worked hard. Chant has certain qualities compared with other forms of music.

The *Śikṣā* continues to stress the importance of the correct use of the hand in recitation. The person who recites the three types of Vedas (*Ṛg Veda*, *Yajur Veda* or *Sāma Veda*) without showing the accents with the hand does not attain divine or subtle energy and cannot be called a *paṇḍit* of the Veda.[16] The *Śikṣā* reiterates that the mind should be focussed and not thinking of other things. The hand should be held in the shape of a fist but neither too open nor too closed. The hand and mouth should be synchronized for it is in this way that the energy of the sound can be obtained. Thus it confirms that the gestures accompanying recitation of the *Yajur Veda* are not only a form of notation but are designed to raise the level of subtle energy and consequently of consciousness.

Having established the correct hand position, the intending student is warned against various other incorrect shapes of the hand. For example, the hand should not be cupped as if holding water, nor should it be shaped like a long boat. It should not be flat nor should it be shaped as if grasping a stick. The fingers should not be separate and at different angles making it look like a swastika but on the other hand it should not be closed like a fist, nor should it look like an axe.[17] Showing the accent with the hand should be like throwing an arrow from a bow. The *Śikṣā* continues the analogy; first the bow string is drawn, and after shooting, the bow string returns immediately to its original place. Similarly, when showing the accents, the hand should move quickly from one place or action to another, thereby stimulating the appropriate energy. As Sidney Allen explains:

> The root *kṣip-* 'to throw', which was used in the phonetic description of the *svarita*, appears also in the gestural terms *urdhva-kṣepa* and *adhaḥ-kṣepa*, 'throwing up' and 'throwing down', referring to the manual gestures accompanying the *udātta* and *anudātta* tones respectively: the gesture for the *svarita* is said in this case to consist of a combination of the two.[18]

Arm and Hand Positions

After preparation for recitation the *Yājñavalkya Śikṣā* describes correct hand positions. In this section of the manual the focus is the relationship of the arm and hand to various energy centres of the body. Why? Because the purpose of recitation using gestures is to purify the subtle body and to generate subtle energy, as compared with coarse physical energy. While the literature of the Vedic period does not refer to *cakras* specifically, we may reasonably deduce that, as they have always been present, they are alluded to in these instructions. The *Śikṣā* explains that the palm of the hand (shaped like a cow's ear) should be turned upwards, facing towards the one who is reciting, and the level of the hand should be between the heart and the tip of the nose. Three body locations are described: *anudātta,* the 'lowered accent', is represented by the heart centre, *udātta*, the 'raised' accent, is at the level of the eyebrows and *svarita*, the intermediary accent, is at the level of the nose.[19]

The *Yājñavalkya Śikṣā*, in its instructions, includes a system of ratios. The span from the tip of the first finger to the tip of the thumb is referred to as *pradesá*. The larger space, to which the span from the tip of the first finger to the tip of the thumb as a unit of measurement (*pradeśa*) relates, is from the brow to the heart.[20] Within this space fingers are used as units of measurement; the distance from *udātta* to *svarita*, that is, from the brow to the nose, is three fingers, and the distance from *svarita* to *anudātta*, from the nose to the heart, is six fingers,[21] making an overall distance from the brow to the heart of nine finger widths. These ratios are said to parallel those between the head and the whole of the body, which in turn represent a relationship between the individual and the universal, a connection between microcosm and macrocosm. Furthermore, it seems that the instructions for the *mudrās* are likely to have been based on a fundamental relationship between head, heart and hand:

> In 1994 I had the opportunity to attend a lecture given by Dr Brian Freeman, an embryologist from Sydney, Australia, at the 4th International Alexander Congress. He was primarily interested in the first nine weeks after the moment of conception ... He explained how the embryo goes through a phase of being extremely curled, in a C-shape. The heart is growing right under the head. The face is resting on the heart. Through the pressure generated between the growing head and the growing heart, the face is sculpted. The brain is tethered into the heart in the most direct way, through the face. As the hands come into form, they too rest in contact with this head/heart centre.[22]

In current practice, movement takes place within a space which is slightly below that just described. The use of *mudrās* in Vedic recitation is not only a form of notation but something more than that. Any gesture of the arm and hand is one which takes perception away from a centre, but certain specifically designed movements can bring a reconnection to that centre. It seems that the concept underlying the relationship between recitation and gesture is to do with a fundamental unity.

Arm and Hand Movements

So far, three basic positions for the arm have been described; in practice, the middle position (*svarita*) is where the right elbow rests on the fist of the left hand, with the hand cupped and shaped like a cow's ear. From this position, the arm may be raised so that the hand is at the level of the shoulder (*udātta*), or it may be lowered so that the hand drops in the direction of the waist (*anudātta*). There may be variations on these basic positions; *udātta* may also be shown by the hand and arm moving across the body to the left side. Similarly an *anudātta* accent may be shown with the hand and arm moving to the right side of the body. *Svarita* is always in the middle position. The choice of movement depends on the context in which the accent occurs. (The final positions for these movements are shown in Plates 1 to 5.)

To explain how this works we may take the archaic or Vedic word for cow or bull which is *go*. Cattle were of central importance in Vedic culture and thought, representing a range of different meanings both literal and symbolic. For instance, while the word *go* can mean cow, it can also mean rays of the sun, stars, milk, nourishment, light or consciousness. The accent given to it is in accordance with the meaning of the word in the context in which it occurs and the hand movement shows the accent with reference to that meaning. Thus, word, meaning and context are co-ordinated with gesture. As a result of this co-ordination, there is the potential for upward movement of energy via three currents of spinal energy (*iḍā*, *piṇgalā* and *suṣumnā*) and the raised level of consciousness and happiness which results.

These kinaesthetics of recitation are dynamic; when an *anudātta* accent is followed by a *svarita* accent, this is shown by a 'scoop' action. In other words, the upturned, cupped hand is turned over and the hand pulled towards the body, turned and moved forward to its original middle position. The movement resembles a 'scooping' action and denotes half the value of an *anudātta* accent and half the value of an *udātta* accent. It cannot be captured on a still slide or illustration as the essential quality is the movement.

Some accents are unmarked in the written form which came later, but are clearly indicated in the very much earlier system of *mudrās*. For example, there is a special instruction for *pracaya*, sometimes described as a sub-type of *svarita*, being an *anudātta* accent which follows a *svarita*. If there is *svarita* at the end of a *mantra*, the hand should indicate the movement smoothly, but if a *pracaya* occurs after a *svarita* at the end of a *mantra*, there will be a downward jerk of the hand, it should fall swiftly. Only the *mudrās* show this situation.

The Hand and Fingers

The manual moves from gestures using arm and hand to those specific movements which involve the hand and fingers. Here the *Śikṣā* describes the way in which the hand should indicate letters which come at the end of a *mantra*. When a *mantra* ends with an '*m*' sound, it should be indicated by a closed fist.

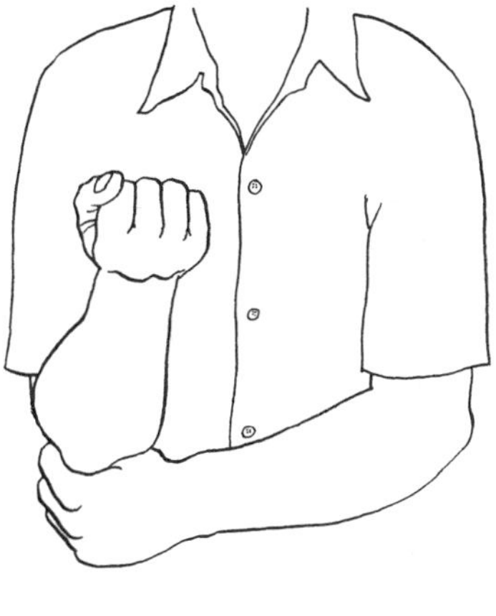

Figure 4.2 ***Mantras*** **ending with an '*m*' sound**

Where a *mantra* ends in a '*p*' sound the five fingertips should join together.

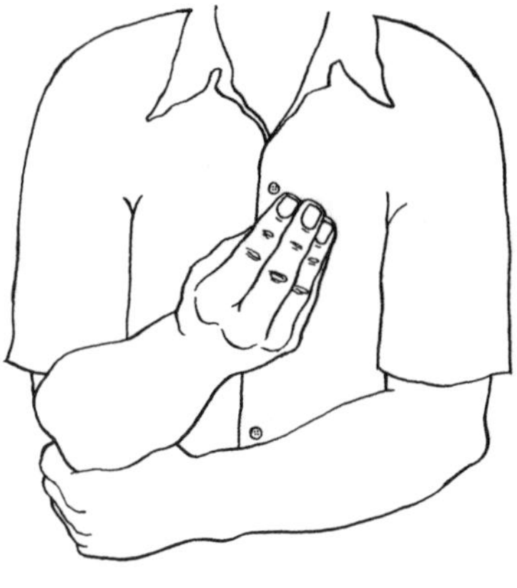

Figure 4.3 ***Mantras*** **ending with a '*p*' sound**

Where the final sound is '*t*' then the thumb and first finger should touch each other.

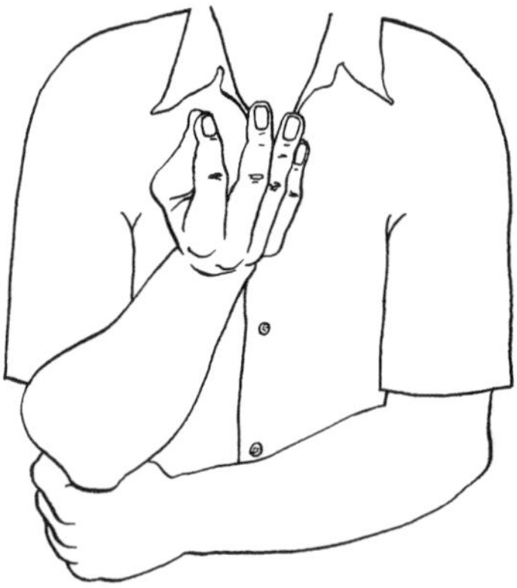

Figure 4.4 ***Mantras*** **ending with a '*t*' sound**

If the *mantra* ends with an '*n*' sound, the top of the first fingernail should touch the thumbnail with the finger on the outside of the thumb.

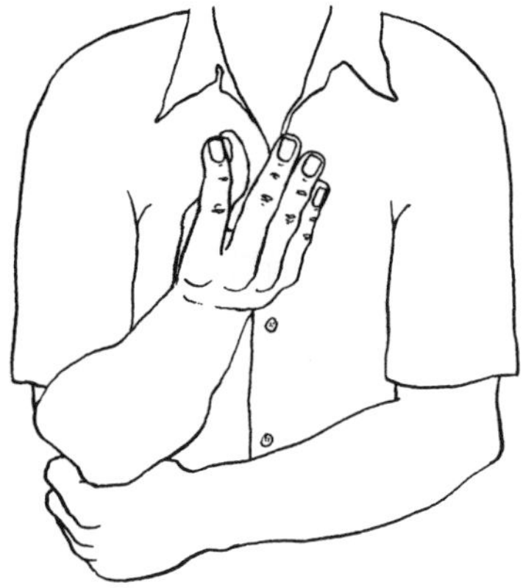

Figure 4.5 ***Mantras* ending with an '*n*' sound**

If a '*k*', '*ṭ*', '*ṅ*' or '*ṇ*' sound ends a *mantra*, the hand should be in the usual shape but with the first finger half-curved.

Figure 4.6 ***Mantras* ending with a '*k*', '*ṭ*', '*ṅ*' or '*ṇ*' sound**

These are eight ways in which a *mantra* may end.

Visargaḥ (*ḥ*), a phonematic emanation said to represent 'unmanifest emitting dynamism'[23] within the process of creation, has an important role to play in pronunciation. The hand is used in three ways to represent *visargaḥ* for this aspirated sound may follow any of the three accents. Usually when *visargaḥ* follows a *svarita* accent, the first and little fingers are straight and the middle two fingers closed.

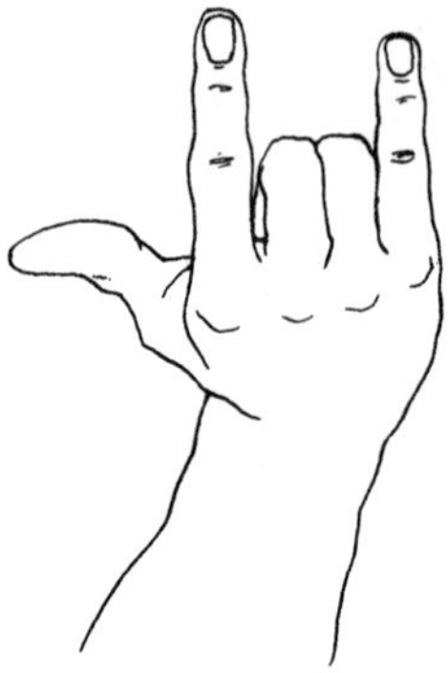

Figure 4.7 ***Visargaḥ*** **following a** ***svarita*** **accent**

When a *visargaḥ* follows an *udātta*, the first finger should be pointed and the remaining fingers closed. This may occur when the arm has moved to the left as well as when it is in the central position.

Figure 4.8 ***Visargaḥ*** **following an** ***udātta*** **accent**

When a *visargaḥ* follows an *anudātta* accent, the little finger should be straight and the remaining fingers closed. This particular hand sign is also used when there is a *visargaḥ* after *pracaya*, a form of *svarita* accent as mentioned above. This *visargaḥ* following an *anudātta* accent may also be shown with the hand moving to the right (see Plates).

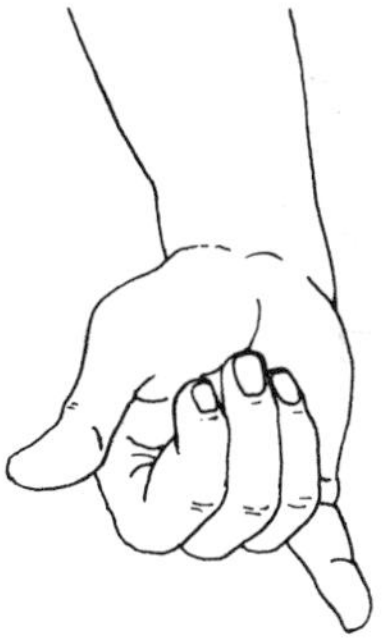

Figure 4.9 ***Visargaḥ* following an *anudātta* accent**

As the purpose of this chapter is not to give a detailed translation of the *Yājñavalkya Śikṣā* but to outline a system of kinaesthetic movements associated with *mantra* recitation, further specific instances for the use of hand signs with *visargaḥ* will not be given.

The technical details involved in the 'science of phonetics' might seem a dry subject but the author of this manual mingles scientific observation with poetic imagery. Thus it says that the hand sign for '*ḥ*' should resemble a young animal with two horns which are not yet fully grown but which are just emerging and therefore are straight and parallel with each other, it should resemble a young girl having two nipples which are not yet fully developed.[24] We do not assume that the *Śikṣā* had only one author or that the visual analogies are as ancient as some of the information in the text, but they do seem to relate to a time when art and science were not conceived of as such separate domains as they are in contemporary Western thought.

The importance given to the use of nasal sounds in the *Yājñavalkya Śikṣā* and in Vedic recitation is of special significance, as has already been discussed in Chapter 2. It is an aspect of sound production which has become considerably modified in classical Sanskrit compared to the language of Vedic *mantra* and has, therefore, become a hidden aspect. One such nasalization is *anusvāra* and occurs when a word ending in '*m*' is followed by a word beginning with a consonant. In this situation the final '*m*' changes to the sound of the nasal consonant of the same family as the following letter, an exception to this rule occurring when the following sound is *ś*, *ṣ*, *s* or *ḥ*.[25] Technically *anusvāra* is described as a nasal sound, an 'after-sound', which is added to a vowel, but in practice it is as if the vowel sound and the nasalization merge together. Some early texts describe this phoneme as *bindu* or 'drop', a term which refers both to its written form, a dot above a vowel, but much more to what it symbolizes, a single point. The written form, which came after the sonic form, is of less concern for the real focus of interest goes back to an earlier time when the oral and aural tradition were paramount; this is a sound which is said to represent the undifferentiated unity of consciousness and which may be experienced as refined knowledge and pure light.[26] It is also said that *bindu* abides in the 'lotus of the heart'.[27] Such sounds in *mantra* recitation are felt to be recurring references to *nāda* (subtle resonance), which is both individual and universal in quality. It is a sound which is inward in direction as compared to the sound of *visargaḥ* which is usually assumed to be outward in expression.[28] In recitation this *anusvāra* is said to be a 'light' (*laghu*) *anusvāra* and is shown by the thumb closing against the side of the first finger.[29]

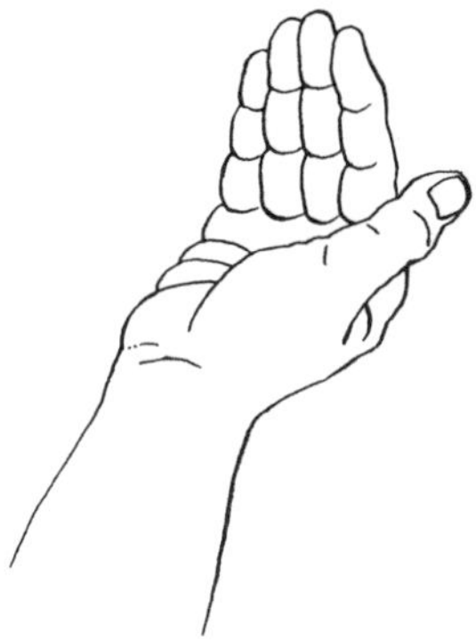

Figure 4.10 ***Anusvāra***

Yajur Veda recitation of the Mādhyandina Branch, to which the *Yājñavalkya Śikṣā* relates, has a number of distinguishing features. One of these is the substitution of '*kh*' for '*ṣ*' so that, for example, the word *puruṣa* reads as *purukha*. The reason why the different traditions of Vedic recitation have distinguishing characteristics has to do with the effectiveness of *mantra*. The analogy given to the writer was that it was like putting one chemical with another: their combination produces a change. The way sounds are put together gives rise to a certain chemistry which produces a result at a subtle level. Another characteristic, which occurs in the context of nasalization, is the pronunciation of *anusvāra* before *ś*, *ṣ*, *s* and *r* as *ghuṃ*.[30] *Ghum* is an internalizing sound with no specific meaning and when it has the length of a long vowel, being two measures in length (*dhīrga ghum*), it is indicated by the first finger pointing with the remaining three fingers closed. There is considerable force attached to this gesture for it is emphatic. The finger is to be 'put forth' with some emphasis. Indeed the gesture should represent the force of the pronunciation of *ghum* which, according to Dr H.R. Sharma, creates an internal sound with a particularly fine vibration 'moving swiftly upward and downward'.[31] In other words, it affects the subtle body and the *cakras*, although, as explained before, *cakras* as such are not mentioned specifically in the four Vedas. It was also explained that this particular use of the *ghum* sound exists in Vedic Sanskrit but not in classical Sanskrit, thus alluding again to an older language from which certain features have become lost during the course of time.

When asked why the instructions in the manual are so specific, it was explained that the *mudrās* are the formulas for movement and sound together and these movements activate the energies of the inner or subtle body. They activate the *nāḍīs* and the area elsewhere referred to as the *ājñā cakra* or 'third eye'. Gross exercise, such as jogging, is for the physical body but these movements are for *prāṇa*, the inner energies. If the grammar changes, the accent will change and consequently the *mudrā* or gesture will change. It is an interaction of three components which affects the nervous system and the subtle body.

It is important to realize that this is a system of sound and movement which preceded yoga, dance and other disciplines. In the *Yājñavalkya Śikṣā*, therefore, there exists a very ancient system for the co-ordination of sound and movement. One might well wonder about the antiquity of this system and the cultural conditions in which it arose and was first practised.

Sāma Veda

Some reference should be made to the *Sāma Veda*, for this Veda is generally considered to be the most important and far-reaching in its implications for indicating the origins of a musical system, that is, a system which makes use of up to seven tones (*svaras*). For it is not only the *Śukla Yajur Vedic* school, to which the Mādhyandina Branch belongs and to which the *Yājñavalkya Śikṣā* specifically refers, which depends upon a system of kinaesthetic movements. The *Nāradīya Śikṣā,* considered to be the most interesting *śikṣā* of those which relate to *Sāma Veda* recitation,[32] also makes reference to gestures.[33] These *mudrās* have the capacity to convey a considerable amount of information with only a few simple movements of the hand. Again, as for the recitation of the *Yajur Veda*, it is the right hand which is used. The individual tones (*svaras*) are indicated by touching the finger joints with the tip of the thumb. The same hand is also used to show melodic sequences, prolongations of tone, and those tones that are to be sung as *kampa* (shaken) – by gliding the thumb over more than one finger joint or by rubbing the side of one of the fingers. Thus, the right hand has the function of showing not only single tones, as for *Yajur Veda* recitation, but also clusters of tones, ornamental tones, and tones that are to be emphasized in some way. It, too, makes use of sound syllables (*stobhas*) not found in later forms of Sanskrit.

As to the origins of the *mudrā* system, it is possible that, as Wayne Howard suggests in his book *Veda Recitation in Vārāṇasī*, it may have been introduced at a time when the tonal system was foreign to the language. The same author orientates his discussion about the use of gestures around the statements of the grammarian Pāṇini, suggesting that Pāṇini's reference to *uccais* (raised) and *nīcais* (lowered), which are usually understood to mean positions in the mouth where sound resonates, actually relate to positions of the right hand during recitation or to bodily postures when recitation is being taught.[34]

Descriptions of *mudrās* used by Nepalese Vājasaneyi and Maharastrian Ṛgvedis resemble those given in the *Yājñavalkya Śikṣā*.[35] The *Nambudiri* branch of *Sāma Veda* recitation, thought by some to be a comparatively later school, also indicates *udātta* with the hand raised and *anudātta* with the hand lowered, but shows *svarita* with the hand to the right and *pracaya* with the hand to the left. The *Nambudiri* teacher emphasizes the learning process by physically manipulating the student's head to an upward position for *udātta*, downward for *anudātta* and sideways for *svarita,* a technique which the writer can confirm from experience. The system expounded in the *Pāṇinīya Śikṣā*, which relates to the *Ṛg Veda*, says that *udātta* is indicated by the top of the thumb held at the root of the index finger, *anudātta* is shown by the thumb touching the middle of the little finger and *svarita* is shown by the thumb touching the middle of the ring finger.[36] The thumb placed on the middle finger indicates *pracaya*. One notable difference here is that the *Yājñavalkya Śikṣā* describes positions for the arm, hand and fingers as a co-ordinated movement. All these descriptions place the hand position for *udātta* as the most upward position. More-detailed discussion regarding *mudrās* for *Sāma Veda* can be pursued further in existing literature on the subject.[37]

As far as *Sāma Veda* recitation is concerned, a function of the gestures may have been their usefulness in a mnemonic capacity. In view of the relative complexity of the melodic line of *Sāma Veda* recitation, it seems that the *mudrās* may have played an essential part in the survival of melodies from ancient times and that hand gestures have been a significant factor in the transmission process of recited Vedas from an ancient period. While it is significant that such a system of accents and gestures which accompany the chant had evolved during a time before 600 BC, there is nothing to show whether the chants were earlier or later than the words of the text. As the hymns (*sāmans*) are mentioned in the *Ṛg Veda*, there is a possibility that they are older and from a source other than the text.

Whether the tradition is that of *Yajur Veda* or *Sāma Veda*, it seems that the strong connection between the language of the phoneticians and the kinaesthetic aspect of the acoustic phenomena implies an interrelatedness so close that they can be perceived as inseparable.

Notes

1 *Encyclopaedia Britannica* vol. 16, p. 21.

2 For further explanation, see D.R. Widdess, 'The Kuḍumiyāmalai Inscription: a source of early Indian music notation', *Musica Asiatic*, 2, 1980, pp. 115-50.

3 See Chapter 5 and also E. te Nijenhuis (1992), *Saṅgītośiromaṇi, Medieval Handbook of Indian Music*, R.J. Brill, Leiden, p. 15.

4 Wayne Howard (1977), Sāmavedic Chant, Yale University Press, New Haven, pp. 78-90 and pp. 106-108.

5 *Yājñavalkya Śikṣā* with commentary by Prakāśaka Dīkśita Kṛṣnacandra Sharma, Vārāṇasī, 1962.

6 Dr H.R. Sharma, Reader and Head of Vedic Studies at Banāras Hindu University, Vārāṇasī.

7 Thomas J. Hopkins (1971), *The Hindu Religious Tradition*, Dickinson, Encino CA, p. 47.

8 The other two *Śikṣā*s are the *Śikṣā* of *Pāṇini* and the *Śikṣā* of *Nārada*.

9 See Chapter 3 on 'Vedic Accents'.

10 Eye focus is a significant topic within different Indian systems. An example occurs in the *Bhagavad Gītā* (6.13) which refers to focus of the eyes as a preliminary approach to meditation, placing the attention on the tip of the nose (which actually means the base of the nose where it joins the upper lip). The *Yājñavalkya Śikṣā* emphasizes that the eyes must be open and focussed on the right hand. There is a verse which occurs in Nandikeśvara's *Abhinaya Darpaṇa* in connection with dance:

> Where the hands go the eyes follow. Where go the eyes, the mind must follow. Where the mind is, there is feeling and where there is feeling there arises sentiment or *rasa*.

The purpose of hand and eye movement co-ordination in dance, which is designed to lead to a particular *rasa* or mood, is quite different from that intended in the recitation of Vedic *mantras* where the purpose of the movements is for purification of body and mind and they are designed to lead to stillness and silence.

11 Mishra, p. 226.

12 The subtle level may also be referred to as the divine level.

13 Swāmī Gambhirānanda (1995 ed.), *Māṇḍūkya Upaniṣad*, Advaita Ashrama, Calcutta, p. 19.

14 Tomatis, p. 165.

15 *Yājñavalkya Śikṣā*, 1:40.

16 This sense of something incomplete is echoed, though with a different sense and purpose, in Indian classical music. It is reminiscent of an often quoted explanation of melodies without ornaments which occurs in the *Nātya Śāstra* ascribed to Bharata and compiled, it is thought, around AD 200.

Like the night without moon, the river without water,
The creeper without blossom,
Like the maiden without adornments is the song without embellishments.

17 *Yājñavalkya Śikṣā*, 1:44.
18 Allen, p. 91.
19 *Yājñavalkya Śikṣā*, 1:51.
20 *Yājñavalkya Śikṣā*, 1:52.
21 *Yājñavalkya Śikṣā*, 1:54.
22 Fertman, p. 17.
23 Padoux, p. 100.
24 *Yājñavalkya Śikṣā*, 1:69.
25 See Appendix 2 for the Sanskrit alphabet and families of sounds.
26 Padoux, p. 273.
27 Padoux, p. 276.
28 There is an inward form of this aspirated sound *ḥ*. The reader should refer to the *Māheśvara Sūtras* of Pāṇini.
29 *Yājñavalkya Śikṣā*, 1:64.
30 Wayne Howard (1986), *Veda Recitation in Vārāṇasī*, Motilal Banarsidass Publishers Pvt. Ltd, Delhi, p. 123.
31 Personal communication from Dr H.R. Sharma, Vārāṇasī, 1998.
32 *Gautamī Śikṣā* and *Lomasī Śīkṣā* also relate to the *Sāma Veda*.
33 *Nāradīya Śikṣā*, 1.6. 1-43 and 1.7. 1-5.
34 Howard, 1986, p. 103.
35 J.E.B. Gray (1959), 'An Analysis of Nambudiri Rgvedic Recitation and the Nature of Vedic Accent', *Bulletin of the School of Oriental and African Studies*, vol. 22, p. 510.
36 Manmohan Ghosh ed. (1938), *Pāninīya Śikṣā*, Asian Humanities Press, Delhi, p. 76 and pp. 43-44.
37 Howard, 1977, pp. 78-90, pp. 106-108, pp. 243-248.

1 *Udātta* accent.

2 *Anudātta* accent.

3 *Svarita* accent.

Mudrās of the *Śukla Yajur Veda* tradition, Mādhyandina Branch demonstrated by Dr H.R. Sharma, Vārāṇasī

Photos: Solveig McIntosh

4 *Udātta* accent on the left side.

5 *Anudātta* accent on the right side.

Mudrās of the *Śukla Yajur Veda* tradition, Mādhyandina Branch demonstrated by Dr H.R. Sharma, Vārāṇasī

Photos: Solveig McIntosh

Chapter 5

Tonal Sequences and Octave Species

When ancient music is compared with modern music, one will no doubt find a gulf which is too vast to span. But if there is anything which gives one some idea of the original music of the human race, it is Eastern music, which still has traces of the ancient music in it.[1]

What was the ancient music? As far as Indian music is concerned we have to learn about earlier stages of development from whatever texts have been handed down and also by identifying fragmentary evidence of earlier traditions which have somehow survived in performance practice. The starting point for this enquiry is the *grāma* system, a science of music whose antiquity has not been ascertained. It is possibly the most ancient known science of music and, we presume, derived from the practice of the art of music of its time. As such it embodies a grammar of music which is true for all times and all places; it is an ancient but universal system. Literally meaning 'a collection or group', a systematic collection of sounds, this science of music comprised three tonal systems out of which scales were evolved. There were *Gāndhāra-grāma, Ṣaḍja-grāma* and *Madhyama-grāma* henceforth abbreviated as *Ga-grāma, Sa-grāma* and *Ma-grāma.* It has been said that *Ga-grāma* belonged in the celestial realm. This may be a euphemism but, whatever we understand the meaning to be, it tells us that, for reasons which are generally left to speculation, it fell into disuse among humanity.

There are three important sources of information about the *grāmas*: the *Śikṣā* attributed to the legendary sage Nārada (*Nāradya Śikṣā*) the *Nātya Śāstra* attributed to Bharata and the *Dattilam* of Dattila. It is the first two to which this chapter refers. The *Nāradīya Śikṣā* was intended as a guide to the correct recitation of the hymns of the *Sāma Veda.* Its authorship and date cannot be accurately verified and, like other writings relating to the Vedic and epic periods, it is a compilation of information accumulated over an indefinite period of time. As it was usual in India to attribute collective works to a single author, it is reasonable to assume that Nārada's *Śikṣā* represents the work of an unknown number of contributors over a considerable period. While its written form is dated from between the first and the fifth centuries AD, it undoubtedly contains material from very much earlier periods of history handed down, it is presumed, by means of an oral tradition. An indication of a history prior to the written form is indicated, for example, by certain words which were in use only during the Vedic period.[2]

Nārada

The topics covered in Nārada's *Śikṣā* which are of relevance in this chapter are those which concern the three basic collections of tones or *grāmas,* twenty-one modes or *mūrchanās*, forty-nine hexatonic scales or *tānas*, and seven *svaras*. The main purpose of this manual is to give instruction on *Sāmavedic* chant but it also includes information on 'secular' (*laukika*) music as well. The complete set of seven *grāma rāgas* associated with the *grāmas* are described in this manual.[3] The *tānas* are allocated, twenty to *Ma-grāma*, fourteen to *Sa-grāma* and fifteen to *Ga-grāma*. The *grāmas* which continued in use were as follows:

Ṣadja grāma: 4 *Sa,* 3 *Ri*, 2 *Ga,* 4 *Ma*, 4 *Pa,* 3 *Dha*, 2 *Ni*

Madhyama-grāma: 4 *Ma,* 3 *Pa,* 4 *Dha*, 2 *Ni,* 4 *Sa,* 3 *Ri*, 2 *Ga*

Figure 5.1 ***Grāmas***

The *śrutis* of each *grāma* add up to 22. The seven scale degrees occur on a pitch continuum which was said to be especially vibrant at 22 points In Western terminology *Ṣadja grāma* starts with *doh* of the Western solfa system of music while *Madhyama-grāma* starts with *fa* of the solfa system.

The *mūrchanā*s were systematic scalar rotations. Each *mūrchanā* consists of seven tones, in a sequence. Interestingly, *mūrchanās* were originally downward rotations and only later became upward movements.[4] These mechanical rotations, using each tone of the basic scale as a starting point, might include either or both of the *sādhāraṇa* tones.[5] Tones could be omitted from a *mūrchanā*; if one or two tones were left out, the *mūrchanā* became a hexatonic or pentatonic *tāna*. There were 49 *tānas*. If there were fewer than five tones, or if tones were not in scale sequence, it became a *kūṭa-tāna*. Bharata and Dattila mention 84 such *tānas*.[6]

The interesting question arises as to whether the purpose of *mūrchanās* was to give tone sequences or interval sequences? They were not used for classifying modes; modal classification based on scales came later. Nor, it seems, were *mūrchanās* attributes of *jātis* (modes), for the *jāti* system is not included in this manual. There were in theory 21 *mūrchanās,* seven for each *grāma,* but in practice 14, each *mūrchanā* being named individually.[7] It has been suggested that one function of the *mūrchanās* may have been as tunings for the arched harp (*vīṇā*) but this is an aspect which is covered more fully by Bharata.

The *Nāradīyā Śikṣā* was primarily a phonetic treatise intended as a guide to the correct recitation of the hymns of the *Sāma Veda*. While the *Ṛg Veda* was recited using up to three accents, the *Sāma Veda*, which is to a large extent the sung version of the *Ṛg Veda,* could use as many as seven tones but in a descending progression.[8] The system of music used for the recitation of *Sāma Veda* falls into seven categories ranging from the use of one tone, two tones, three tones up to seven tones, referred to as *ārcika*, *gāthika*, *sāmika*, *svarāntara*, *oḍava*, *ṣāḍava*, *sampūrṅa*.[9] In practice there are more hymns which use three tonal regions or accents than use six and seven tones. Some say that this represents a logically progressive development in the use of musical scale; however, it is more likely that the use of varying numbers of tones represents different musical formulae, for this was the music of *mantra* recitation, often referred to as 'music of the Path', a form of *mārga saṅgīta*. It was a music with a well-defined set of rules and as such was highly symbolic. The descending nature of the melodic movement is conducive to bringing the mind and emotions to a state of peace, though these musical formulae were not the same as melody, for they contained no elements of self-expression but were instruments for the attainment of something beyond the mundane level of worldly existence. There is nothing to say that these formulae or chants evolved at the same time as the words, nor were they necessarily later than the words; as incantations made up of the archaic *grāma* they could be older and from a source other than the text. It seems that there was a general tendency for ancient cultures to use musical progressions which descended from high to low tones.

The seven tones of the descending scale, a different idea from the descending patterns of the musical formulae referred to above, are named in this *śīkṣā* as: *kruṣṭa* (loud), *prathama* (first), *dvitīya* (second), *tṛtīya* (third), *caturtha* (fourth), *mandra* (low), *atisvāra* (the last). This is an ancient terminology which can also be found in older Vedic auxiliaries such as the *Taittirīya Prātiśākhya*.[10] From a practical point of view, the first tone of the descending scale is the tone produced by simply blowing into the flute. The tone produced by covering the first hole is *prathama*.[11] Both the flute and lute were said to accompany the singing of *sāmans* (hymns).

However, in *Sāma Veda* the intervals are not fixed, for in *Sāma Veda* seven levels are not differentiated by *śruti* intervals as they are in singing, where there are seven *svaras* or tones. It is also said that it was with the increased use of the lute (*vīṇā*) that there emerged an ascending order of tones referred to as *ṣadja*, *ṛṣabha*, *gāndhāra*, *madhyma*, *pañcama*, *dhaivata*, and *niṣāda*. This was the secular scale (the *laukika* scale).

As for the three accents, these tones were attributed with various qualities which related the seven *svaras* to various colours, castes, animal cries, bodily locations, seers and deities. '*Ṣaḍja* screams the peacock, but the bull roars *ṛṣabha*, the goat bleats *gāndhāra*, and the crane cries *madhyama*. In springtime the cuckoo whistles *pañcama*, while the horse makes the sound of *dhaivata*, and the elephant *niṣāda*.'[12] If they are understood to represent different qualities perceived intuitively and expressed in a language unfamiliar to us, we may appreciate their meaning. If we also consider contemporary electronic technology, which has shown that there is far more music underlying some of the sounds we hear made by animals and birds than at first appears, we may find that this intuition is confirmed. A progressively slowed-down digital version of a fragment of a simple English blackbird song reveals, at each stage, a distinct tune with clear pitch organization and even ornamentation of some tones. This is interesting from another point of view for it reveals that melodies are intrinsic in nature, they are the raw material from which scales can be abstracted.

At a time when the male Brahmin community was responsible for formalized music, the recitation of the Vedas, there existed other musical forms, secular art forms not bound by the occult framework of Vedic singing. In these forms, which included dance and the playing of musical instruments, women played a significant role.[13] By the end of the Vedic period the *sargama* system as it is known today had evolved.[14]

Nārada mentions seven scalar modes (*grāma rāgas*)[15] based on the tones of the two principal *grāmas* and from this evidence it has been deduced that the original seven *grāma rāgas* were the predominant modes in musical practice during the middle years of the first millennium AD. Interestingly this ancient system of *grāma rāgas* can be found described in *Suishu*, a Chinese document relating to the Northern Zhou dynasty around AD 568.[16] They can also be found portrayed in notation in the Kuḍumiyāmalai rock inscription near Puḍokattai in Tamil Nādu where they have been dated to the seventh and eighth century. Inscribed on the wall of a temple, these seven melody forms in musical notation represent each of the basic *grāma rāgas* and, as such, are an exceptional example of a recording of a musical system. Multiplicity being one of the laws of creation, the number of *grāma rāgas* increased during the first millennium to 32 (or 33) which then required some form of classification. This was done according to five different categories of style, the *gītis*. However, this early *grāma* system was not the same as the early modal (*jāti*) system of Bharata which was in use around AD 500 though no doubt had a much earlier source. These *jātis* later evolved into what are now known as *rāgas*. It would seem that these two documents of musical theory and practice are likely to represent separate streams of musical influence which during the course of time merged and subsequently appeared in the textual tradition.

There are other interesting points of comparison between the documents attributed to Nārada and Bharata. Tonal quality is discussed by Nārada in terms of a system of five *śrutis*. This set of five *śrutis* comprise: *dīptā*,[17] having the quality of brightness or intensity; *āyatā*, an extended tone; *karuṇā*, subdued; *mṛdu*, soft; and *madhyama* or moderate.[18] However, these *śrutis*, which represent tonal qualities and are presented in connection with the *Sāmavedic* scale, are a different set of criteria from the set of 22 *śrutis* described by Bharata. In the context of tonal quality Bharata speaks of three *śrutis* – *madhyā* (the central tone), *mṛdu* (a lowered tone) and *āyatā* (a 'stretched' or extended tone in a higher register) – which suggests a derivation from the three Vedic accents.[19] It shows, too, how one musical form influences another. As far as the set of 22 *śrutis* is concerned it is easy to see that an octave can be divided into many more than 22 divisions. This strongly indicates some other reason for dividing a whole into this number. While the 22 *śrutis* relate to microtonal distinctions between tones, as the *grāma* system shows, the five *śrutis* described by Nārada appear to relate to tonal quality or timbre rather than to precise measures of pitch. Although we do not know at what stage this practice was adopted, it was clearly of importance as the *Śikṣā* informs us that a person not familiar with the five *śrutis* was not worthy of being considered a teacher.[20] We can only speculate as to why there were two different *śruti* systems and what their relationship to each other was historically.

The evidence for a coherent musical system may appear confusing unless one can accept that there may be instances of different levels of meaning. A complete theory of music, after all, consists of its grammar, science of acoustics, history, literature, iconography, psychology and philosophy.[21] *Grāmas*, for example, which at one level are collections of available tones rather than musical scales, at another level could be described as archetypal forms. At one time the word *yama*, was used for a tone. Later, in the *Prātiśākhya* and *Śikṣā* period, the word used for a tone was *svara.*[22] The word *yama*, with its connotations of human soul, suggests that the *grāma* system may originally have been as much a philosophical system as a musical one. The reference to three *grāmas* comprising seven *svaras*, another instance of 'threeness' and 'sevenness', suggests that the system refers as much to universal principles as it does to musical practice. Octaves, after all, are series of expansions and not linear at all. We may also note that in philosophical terms the number 49 (*tānas*) represents the cosmological wheel and the number 21 (*mūrchanā*) represents the earth component of the cosmos.[23] Nor is it surprising that Nārada's *Śikṣā* should mention both a descending and an ascending scale. Indian philosophy teaches that there is a circulation of energies, from *Brahmā* to creation, from fine to gross, and then from coarse to fine in which mankind participates either unconsciously or consciously.[24] The existence of two scale forms could be understood to be an expression of a fundamental process.

As far as the *śrutis* are concerned, it is obvious that many more than 22 divisions of an octave can be distinguished by the ear. Twenty-two *śrutis* and seven tones, the association with the mathematical axiom *pi* or 22/7 thought of as a transcendental number cannot be ignored. Although it is not the purview of this book to explore these ideas further, it is nevertheless clear that the ancient science of music is much more than a grammar or practical method. *Śruti* is an expression of physical, physiological, emotional and esoteric aspects of music. If the discussion is brought into the domain of the twenty-first century the emphasis on speed in some contemporary instrumental playing, which entertains the public, is often so fast that it is not possible to develop and shape the 22 *śrutis* of the old Indian scale system. Such developments bring about interesting changes but in so doing something has been lost.

Bharata

The *Nāṭya Śāstra,* attributed to the sage Bharata and dated around AD 200, is a sizeable treatise on dramaturgy which also discusses certain fundamental principles of music, including music used for the purpose of drama, the word *nāṭya* being a concept comprising drama, dance and music. This is not the first occasion when music and drama are referred to in the same context. There are others references one of which is the *Aṣṭādhyāyī* of Pāṇini, compiled around 600 BC, where music is referred to as comprising dance, song, instrumental music and stage-acting.[25] Nor is it generally considered that Bharata's work is the earliest record of organized and systematized music, as these are to be found in Egyptian and Sumerian texts dated around 3000 BC. Whatever its more exact antiquity, this is an Indian source which gives detailed information on different aspects of an ancient musical system in relation both to ritual and to incidental music.[26]

The treatise takes a form which was a characteristic style for imparting important information, that of a dialogue between a supposed authority, Bharata, and learned enquiry, the sages. A similar style was adopted in the *Upaniṣads*. By means of this method of communication, Bharata, drawing on material for this drama from the ancient scriptures, the Vedas, teaches the whole of *Brahmā's* divine creation to mankind for it is said that the original work was composed by God, *Brahmā*, for celestial immortals ruled by Indra.

It is not possible to ascertain just how ancient the knowledge expounded in the *Nātya Śāstra* is; just as there was language before the explanation of grammatical rules, so there was music and drama before the written treatises on the subject. Although acclaimed as a fifth Veda, the *Nātya Śāstra* was accessible to all four castes, an indication as to why this work is inclusive of non-Vedic aspects of music. In this context it should be remembered that the original concept of the caste system was not hierarchical as it has subsequently become; the four castes represented four professions, each essential for the proper conduct of life on earth. Like the *Nāradīya Śikṣā*, this early written authority on the tradition of music in India speaks of two *grāma*s, known as *Sa-grāma* and *Ma-grāma*. At first sight this would seem to suggest that the system of *grāmas* might be of a later date than the work of the grammarians (*c.* 600 BC) but the *Nātya Śāstra* is undoubtedly a compilation from much earlier sources whose origin is obscure. An important passage in the *Ṛk Prātiśākhya* indicates that the system of *grāmas* was in existence around 400 and 500 BC. But this again is written evidence based on knowledge which could be very much older.[27]

From this account, however, we can begin to see how remarkable the system of *grāmas* is. At one level it is a science or theory constructed on the basis of the art or practice of music at the time which embodies the essence of the science of musical scales and, we may conclude, is for the sake of classification and explanation. Just as *sūtras* are short, concise statements or rules from which much more expansive concepts may be deduced, similarly *grāma* is an economical system which represents a grammar of musical scales based on universal principles. It is not proposed to go into every detail of the musical system given in the *Nātya Śāstra*, as this has been discussed at some length by other contemporary authors, but a general summary of some of the salient points will be made.[28]

The *grāmas*, as a grammar of music, serve two distinct purposes. The first of these is that it is a system based on two main consonances. By means of a technique known as *sāraṇā catuṣṭaya*, Bharata calculated the intervals of the tones of each *grāma.*[29] *Sa-grāma* is based on *Sa-Pa,* a perfect fifth consonance consisting of 13 *śruti* intervals. Within this *grāma Ri-Dha* (2-6), *Ga-Ni* (3-7), *Ma-Sa* (4-8) are all 13 *śruti* intervals. *Ma-grāma*, on the other hand, is based on *Ri-Pa,* a perfect fourth consonance. This apparently simple statement opens up a vast realm of musical implication. The first observation which emerges is that while in *Sa-grāma Sa-Pa* is a consonant interval, *Ri-Pa* is not consonant because the 3 *śruti* interval between *Sa* and *Ri* in *Sa-grāma* makes *Ri-Pa* a 10 *śruti* interval. In *Ma-grāma,* however, *Sa-Pa* is not a consonant interval because the *Pa* of *Ma-grāma* is 12 *śrutis* from *Sa* (it should be 13 to be consonant) but the relationship of *Ri to Pa* is 9 *śrutis* which is a consonant interval. In other words, we see that the difference between the *Sa-Pa* interval in *Sa-grāma* and in *Ma-grāma* is just one *śruti.* This comprises the *pramāna-śruti* or the standard *śruti.* In mathematical language this is represented as 81/80 which is referred to as the 'comma of Didymus' in the Greek system, one of the greatest mysteries of the science of sound.

The 'comma of Pythagoras', as it is also called, is a phenomenon explored by ancient music-philosophers, the Chinese using the ratios 1:3 and 3:1 and the Greeks using the cycle of fifths in order to evolve a system of 12 consecutive tones are two well-known examples. According to the Greek system the cycle of 12 perfect fifths did not complete a cycle of seven octaves, but slightly exceeded it, giving rise not to a repetitive cycle but to an upward spiral which was consequently conceived of as a symbol of regeneration. Whichever method was used it was found that there was always a discrepancy in the completion of octaves. This discovery is wide-ranging in that it is a phenomenon which can be seen, for example, in the days of the year which do not work out exactly each year and consequently give rise to a situation which is resolved by a periodic leap year which has an 'extra' day. What is impressive about the *grāma* system expounded in the *Nāṭya Śāstra* is that this subtle interval is expressed with such simplicity.

The discrepancy between *Ma-grāma* and *Sa-grāma* established the standard measurement of a single *śruti*, equivalent to a 'comma'. As has been shown already, the 22 *śrutis* focus themselves around the seven tonal centres or points of resonance of the collection of tones referred to as *grāma.* Looked at from a horizontal point of view, the *Nāṭya Śāstra* reflects the doctrine that *svaras* are primary intervals with *śrutis* as secondary pitch positions which could be perceived and demonstrated in association with a particular *svara.* Thus *svaras* were said to contain or possess a stipulated number of *śrutis.*[30]

From a vertical point of view, each tone of a *grāma* is a focus of energy representing a starting point, the fundamental or first harmonic, for the harmonic series. The first overtone is the second harmonic, the only difference between harmonics and overtones being in their numbering. This linear harmonic series occurs as a natural phenomenon in nature. The following illustration covers four octaves and shows that the perfect fifth interval occurs more often than does the octave.

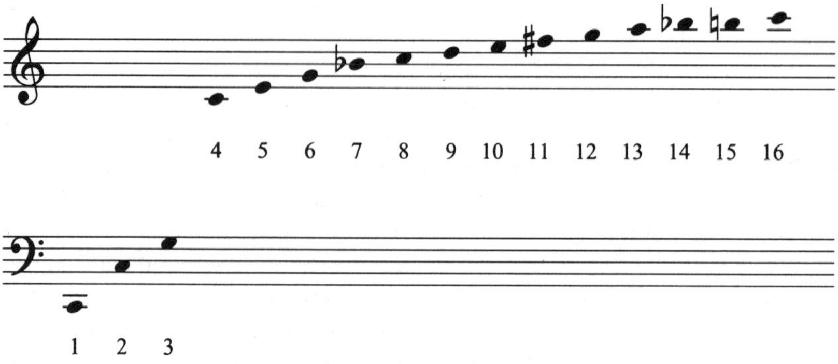

Figure 5.2 Harmonic series

The second main purpose has to do with the classification of musical scales. The *grāma* system is sufficiently versatile for the relationship of *Ma-grāma* and *Sa-grāma* to be discussed in terms of *mūrchanās*, as the former can be derived from the latter by changing some of the tones. It is explained as follows. If the *Sa* of *Sa-grāma* is called *Ma* and the *Ga* of *Sa-grāma* is increased by two *śruti*s and called *Dha*, a particular *mūrchanā* (rotation) of *Sa-grāma* gives *Ma-grāma*. Similary *Ma-grāma* can be obtained by means of a particular rotation of *Sa-grāma* where *Dha* is lowered by two *śruti*s and called *Ga*. When approached in this way one *grāma* is a *mūrchanā* of the other. It has been suggested, moreover, that this system of rotation gives rise to all the musical scales of Indian music.[31]

Svara sādhāraṇa is another feature of these early scale systems. It means 'overlapping' and involves the raising of the flattened third by two *śrutis* and the raising of the seventh scale degree also by two *śrutis* (*Ga* flat or *Ni* flat). These additional tones, introduced into a system of seven tones, were called *kākali niṣāda* and *antara gāndhāra*. In this way the *śrutis* of *Ga* (the third scale degree) combine with those of *Ma* (the fourth scale degree) and those of *Ni* (the seventh scale degree) overlap with those of *Sa* (the tonic). Theoretically this brought the number of available tones to nine. While the reason for this introduction is the subject of considerable discussion, we may note that both *Ga* and *Ni* function as leading tones in two separate tetrachords; they are points of tension which require resolution. (Tetrachords are tone sequences built between the intervals of a fourth.)

Tetrachordal scale construction was the underlying principle in ancient Greek music, one tetrachord descending a fourth from the keytone, and the other ascending a fourth, making a heptatonic, or seven-tone scale. A similar concept exists in ancient Indian music theories, as has been discussed in Chapter 3 on Vedic accents, for if the three accents of Vedic recitation are repeated in two different registers, a scale of tones emerges.[32] In the ancient *gāndharva* system, the altered third and seventh scale degrees were the only additional tones allowed, though they were not given independent status but considered as modified forms. This merging of tonal realms has an analogy in the overlapping seasons as Bharata describes:

> There is a time of year when one feels cold in the shade but sweats in the sun; this is the period when spring cannot be said to have not arrived but winter is not fully over.[33]

The significance of this modification of the seven-tone system should not be overlooked either from a physiological point of view, with its inherent potential for heightened aesthetic experience, or from a historical perspective. The importance of the seventh scale degree, *Ni*, is mentioned by Nārada who refers to 'comings [from] and goings [to] Ni'. In ancient sources such as the Kuḍumiyāmalai inscription and in a very much later work, the *Saṅgīta Ratnākara*, there are more melodic movements that originate from or arrive at this tone than any other.[34] The seventh frequency and its harmonics are dissonant with the fundamental. Scientifically, we may note that certain select vibrations, tuned to the seventh harmonic, have a neurological effect as they excite and amplify bio-energies. Aesthetically we may hear this idea developed in classical vocal music. The Ḍāgar style of singing *dhrupada*, for example, places considerable emphasis on very subtle renditions of any of the tones depending on the aesthetic requirements of the *rāga* being performed. The seventh scale degree is no exception, for the tradition teaches that an artist should be able to demonstrate several shades of intonation for this tone in performance practice.

Bharata refers to *gāndharva* music. As with so many Sanskrit terms this was a word used in two senses – general and specific. In general, all formalized music was known as *gāndharva* and was even considered a subsidiary Veda. More specifically, it meant music that was intended for *adṛṣta phalla*, for obtaining the unseen result, for religious merit or praising the gods. This was a highly grammatical music and in the *Nāṭya Śāstra* was used in a specific sense.[35] The main components of *gāndharva* were *svara*, *tāla* and *pada* (tone, time and word or syllable) with specific rules for obtaining unseen spiritual results. Vocal music, *vīṇā* and flute (*vaṃṣa*) formed the triad of *gāndharva* music with the main emphasis on vocal music and with *vīṇā* and flute lending a special harmony. *Deśī* (regional) music, on the other hand, was grammatically freer and was meant for 'pleasing the hearts of men'. Music which was merely for entertainment in certain parts of the drama is referred to as *gāna* in this treatise.

It has been said that at the beginning of the classical period, which is dated at around 600 BC, there evolved a new modal or *jāti* type of music which was mainly connected with the performance of drama.[36] Whether this is an accurate description of events or not, the main form of *gāndharva* music, as described by Bharata, was *jāti*. *Jāti* was defined as a pattern of tones designed to give aesthetic delight which in turn gave rise to well-being and happiness at all levels of human experience.[37]

Indeed, one of the main contributions of Bharata was a detailed description of *jāti* music, for the seven modes mentioned by Nārada, which formed a modal system, were not the same as the *jāti* system. Literally meaning 'class or kind', they were derived from the *mūrchanās*. Bharata mentions eighteen *jātis*, seven derived from *Sa-grāma* and eleven derived from *Ma-grāma*. Four from *Sa-grāma* and three from *Ma-grāma* were known as 'pure', while the remainder were the result of a fusion of two or more *jātis* and were known as 'impure' or 'modified' forms. Similar to the system described by Nārada was the establishment of seven pure forms before modified forms could be derived. From the basic 'pure' *jātis* there was the possibility for any number of other varieties to be derived for such a process of growth is a naturally occurring one.

The concept of music as a 'continuum with scale and tune at its extremes' is a useful one.[38] The 'tune' aspect of early music is discussed in terms of *gāna* or *gīta,* that combination of sounds which pleases the mind and emotions, which creates mood and has an aesthetic aspect, whereas speech-song serves a different purpose having recitative value. A *jāti* or modal type, on the other hand, was a melodic idea which offered potential for improvisation. It was defined by certain rules of musical grammar. These took the form of ten characteristics or *lakṣaṇas* and enabled the expression of particular dramatic situations and emotional states. A *jāti*, for instance, had to have accepted stages or pauses – *nyāsa,* being the final tone on which a song ends, *apanyāsa,* the tone on which the middle portion of the song ends, and *sanyāsa.* It had to have *aṁśa*, a vital tone which was the most common tone or key-tone, showing the extent to which a tone may be used within a register.[39] Something of the idea underlying the use of *aṁśa* has been replaced in the performance of *rāga* by the use of one prominent tone known as *vādi*. Phrases began only on a specific tone, *graha*. The frequent and infrequent use of tones (*bahutva* and *alpatva*), the emphasis on the upper (*tāra*) and lower (*mandra*) ranges, the availability of five, six or seven tones – all these influenced the formation of *jāti*. So too did *ṣāḍavita*, when a tone from a seven-tone scale was omitted and six tones were used, and *auḍuvita* when two tones were omitted and only five tones were used. To this standard collection of characteristics another important concept was included, *antaramārga* (internal pathway), taking the form in performance as *saṅgati* or *sañcāri* indicating frequent movement between two *svaras*. Together these formed an important set of instructions for bringing scalar material to life, for engendering tune from scale.

The study of interval is the study of one of the hidden aspects of music; the way in which tones and intervals are organized in *rāgas* influences the aesthetic effect. It underlies the way particular *rāgas* are appropriate to different times of the day and seasons of the year. Within the *jāti* system, intervals were based on *śruti* measurements and consequently presented the listener with a different sound experience from equal temperament now in use in Western music with its attendant underlying stress component. It has been suggested that a move away from pure tuning towards equal tuning not only represents a loss of spiritual connection but is also associated with the development of technology and material progress.

Observation of recent developments in aspects of Indian music at the same time as a rapid development in technology in India would seem to support this view. For this reason it is worth rediscovering what the ancient systems of music offered.

While a system of tonal characteristics (*lakṣaṇa*), as described by Bharata, is not mentioned in Nārada's *śikṣā*, the basic modal system based on the *grāmas* developed certain qualities. Two verses illustrate this:

> Domination of *gāndhāra*, departure and arrival of *niṣāda*, weakness of *dhaivata* are the reasons why it is called *madhyama grāma*. That is pointed out as the *ṣaḍjagrāma* where *niṣāda* is slightly touched, *gāndhāra* is in predominance and *dhaivata* vibrates.[40]

As we said previously, Nārada's work is a compilation from an oral tradition, making it seem highly probable that this description represents a later addition to an existing musical system. Scholars admit that the chronological relationship with the *jāti* system propounded by Bharata is not clear. It is conceivable that the music for the *Nāṭya Śāstra*, the *grāmas* and *jātis* with their philosophical, esoteric and musical aspects, were the remnants of a previous system.

It can be said that these *jātis* were not yet *rāgas* but contained the early stages of the *rāga* system. It is also true that by the time the *Saṅgīta Ratnākara* was compiled in the thirteenth century, the *grāma* system was no longer understood.[41] Though at one time the *grāma* system served to regulate the organization of *svara*, *śruti*, *mūrchanā*, *tāna*, *jāti* and *rāga*,[42] the method of obtaining 22 *śruti*s within an octave was later abandoned, and the relationship of *Sa-grāma* and *Ma-grāma* through *mūrchanā*s was lost. Today *rāga* has an individual identity; everything is based on *Sa* as a tonic. When *Sa-grāma* was taken to represent a diatonic scale, the concept of *Ma-grāma* was abandoned and Indian music became established on this basis. As a consequence, two *rāgas* such as *Jayjavanti* and *Hamīr* are now heard as separate, whereas previously these two melody forms could have been heard as the same *jāti* operating in *Sa-grāma* and *Ma-grāma* because in terms of phrases they are the same.[43] Thus *Sa-grāma* and *Ma-grāma* came to be thought of as a duality whereas, as has been shown, they were in fact two elements or components of a single whole.

> An inquiry into the ethos and structure of some of the oldest music of which there is any record is not a mere piece of antiquarianism; it throws that sort of light on the music of modern India which a knowledge of the geology of a country throws upon its scenery.[44]

Notes

1 Khan, 1977, p. 19.
2 Singh, 1995, p. 9.
3 *Nāradīya Śikṣā*, 1.4.5-11.
4 Bharata, *Nāṭya Śāstra*, 28.32.

5 Literally 'overlapping' tones which in practice meant raising the *Ga* flat (the third scale degree) and *Ni* flat (the seventh scale degree) by two *śrutis* – *sādhāraṇa*.

6 Mukhund Lath, (1978), *A Study of Dattilam*, Impex, Delhi, p. 250 and Lewis Rowell (1992), *Music and Musical Thought in Early India*, The University of Chicago Press, Chicago, p. 161.

7 From the meaning of the root *murchā* in the *Dhātu Pāṭhaḥ* the meaning 'rising, increase, growth, height and high degree' is derived (Monier-Williams, p. 1165) Elsewhere the meaning 'modulation, melody, a regulated rise or fall of sounds through the *grāma* or musical scale' is given (Monier-Williams, p. 823). Bharata also describes *mūrchanās* but they are named slightly differently. The root *tan* conveys the sense of that which spreads or expands.

8 'Sung' in the context of recitation implies an 'intoned' form of singing.

9 Singh, 1995 p. 11.

10 *Taittirīya Prātiśākhya*, 23:16,17.

11 *Nāradīya Śikṣā*, 1.5.1-2.

12 *Nāṭya Śāstra*, 1.5.3-4.

13 Singh, 1994, cites many examples.

14 Singh, 1995, p. 11.

15 *Nāradīya Śikṣā*, 1.4.5-11.

16 D.R. Widdess (1994), *Rāgas of Early Indian Music: Modes, Melodies and Musical Notations from the Gupta period to c.1250,* The Clarendon Press, Oxford, p. 15 and Rowell (1992), p. 173.

17 *Dīpta* is the word used for pitch in the *Taittirīya Prātiśākhya* which pertains to the *Kṛṣṇa Yajurveda*. The *Prātiśākhyas* are said to precede the *śikṣās* and while the former deals with Vedic phonetics and to some extent with music, the latter deals mainly with Vedic phonetics and also some music. Also Singh (1995), pp. 7-8.

18 *Nāradīya Śikṣā*,1.7.9-18.

19 Bharata, *Nāṭyaśāstra*, 29:38b, 39, 40.

20 *Nāradīya Śikṣā*, 1.7.9.

21 Swāmī Prajñānānanda (1973), *Historical Development of Indian Music*, Firma K.L. Mukhopadhyay, Calcutta, p. 30.

22 *Svara* has other meanings. See Glossary and Index.

23 Feuerstein, Kak and Frawley, p. 20.

24 The Advaita system of Indian Philosophy.

25 V.S. Agrawala, (1953), *India as Known to Pāṇini*, University of Lucknow, IV.3.129.

26 Curt Sachs (1943), *The Rise of Music in the Ancient World – East and West,* W.W. Norton, New York, pp. 58-59.

27 Strangways, p. 114.

28 The reader should refer to Lath, *A Study of Dattilam*, 1978; Rowell, *Music and Musical Thought in Early India*, 1992; and Widdess, *The Rāgas of Early Indian Music*, 1994.

29 See Chapter 5 on 'Tonal Sequences' – '*catus*' means a group of 'four' and *prahāra* means stroke referring to the practice of *vīṇā* playing. See Singh, 1995, p. 36 and Prajñānānanda, pp. 24-25.

30 Others, for example Dattilam and Mataṅga, thought *śrutis* gave rise to *svaras*.

31 Precise instructions were given by Bharata (as well as later writers) for changing the tuning of a *vīṇā* from a *Sa-grāma mūrchanā* to a *Ma-grāma mūrchanā*; these instructions included playing of *tānas* as well as *kūṭa-tānas*. This, too, it seems, was the ancient system, where *śruti* intervals were predetermined for obtaining different scales and were the basis for the formation of *rāgas*. *Nāṭya Śāstra*, 28, and Prem Lata Sharma (2000), *Indian Aesthetics and Musicology*, Amnaya Prakasana, Vārānasī p. 116.

32 See Chapter 3 on 'Vedic Accents'.

33 *Nāṭya Śāstra*, 28:34.

34 Widdess, 1994, p. 122.

35 Nārada refers to *gāndharva* but only to analyse a possible etymology of the word: 'The meaning of the term *gāndharva* is this: GĀ, say the wise, means "to be sung"; DHA, the proper playing of the instrumental strokes (*dhātus*); and VĀ, the playing of the instrumental music (in general)' (1.4.12).

36 Prajñānānanda, p. 73.

37 Singh, 1995, p. 39.

38 H. Powers, 'India', in *New Grove Dictionary of Music and Musicians*, Macmillan Publishers Ltd. London, 1980, vol. 9, p. 68.

39 During the course of time, *aṁśa* became a tonic or fundamental reference-tone for the construction of melodies. By sustaining this tone, together with its consonant fourth and fifth, it became established as the drone accompaniment for contemporary Indian music.

40 *Nāradīya Śikṣā*, 1.4.7-8.

41 Prem Lata Sharma, 2000, p. 118.

42 Sharma and Shringy, 1991, vol. 1, p. 167 footnote.

43 Personal communication from Dr Ritwik Sanyal, Banāras Hindu University, December 1997.

44 Strangways, p. 246.

Chapter 6
Song Forms

Music according to the ancient people was not a mechanical science or art; music was the first language.[1]

All over the world the history of song is a vast and ancient subject. To sing and to make music must be one of the deepest of human loves. Therefore the impulse to make melodious sounds is fundamental and the human feeling for organization and the desire to construct is innate. The Indian tradition, of course, is no exception and consequently, in the history of song, as it is known at present, there have been many different kinds of song forms. To describe something of what is known of the history of these forms is dry academia compared with the impulse which lies behind their creation. This is especially so when their sound, which is all-important, cannot be conveyed through the written word. Nevertheless, such a description is attempted here both from the point of view of a historical perspective and as a framework for understanding contemporary classical music. We can summarize the situation by saying that the evolution of current classical styles of music in northern India progressed from Vedic hymns through folk music and devotional music to classical forms. But this brief resumé is only a glimpse, for songs arise and disappear according to the needs of people at any one time.

Because of the many different kinds of songs or ways of constructing musical forms that exist in the Indian tradition, there is an array of words to describe them. As with other terms in music literature, there is also a certain amount of overlapping of meaning. At one time, it seems, there were some specific rules for the different types of song but the distinctions have become blurred. In the case of Vedic recitation both the words *sāmagāna* and *sāmagīti* have been used, just as the words recitation, song, chant and hymn are used interchangeably in translation. Moreover, the songs of the *Ṛg Veda* have also been referred to as *gīti*, *gāthā* and *gāyatra*. Generally, *gāthās* were songs sung on occasions of ceremonies and festivals.[2] Similarly, the words *gītā* and *saṅgīta* are frequently used in the same sense to denote the art of music in general, though the term *saṅgīta* at one time referred specifically to the combination of three arts, vocal, instrumental and dance. But *saṅgīta* became a twofold concept: that music which was dedicated to *Brahmā* was *mārga*, while that which entertained the people was known as *deśī*.[3] Consequently, sometimes it is asked what are the differences between *gīti*, *gītā*, *gāna*, *gītaka*, *gāndharva*, *sāma* and so on, all of which mean song in one form or another?

Taking *gīti* as a starting point, some aspects of the various forms which have been in practice and which have exerted an influence over contemporary performance will be discussed. *Mantra* recitation, as has been established earlier, is of an antiquity which cannot be calculated. When we hear it said, therefore, that *mantra* recitation is *gīti* in the form of *sāma* (the term used for the recitation of *Sāma Veda*) the implication is that *gīti* is a very old term referring, it is presumed, to set melodic patterns. Nowadays there are considered to be two broad categories of *gīti*: one refers to the way in which a text is set and the other refers to style in general. The situation seems incongruous, in that the term apparently means two different things.

On the basis of syllable and rhythm, the way a text is set, there are four varieties of *gīti* technically referred to as *māgadhī, ardhamāgadhī, sambhāvitā* and *pṛthulā*. The particular feature of these *gītis* was that the singer was required to keep the number of beats constant in all the lines regardless of the fact that the number of syllables in each line was different. One explanation of *māgadhī gīti* is that the first line had few syllables and was sung in slow tempo, the second had more syllables and was sung in medium tempo and in the third line there were again more syllables and these had to be sung in fast tempo. Another explanation is that in *māgadhī gīti* words were repeated in their entirety, whereas in *ardhamāgadhī gīti* repetitions were in half the time. The *sambhāvitā gīti* is understood to have many short syllable letters while *pṛthulā gīti* is rich in sounds using long syllables. Each of these *gītis* has been described as belonging to a particular *mārga*.[4] They were originally described by Bharata who said of these *gītis,* elsewhere referred to as *gītaka*, that they were not to be used in stage songs (*dhruvās*) but only in the ritual music performed during the prelude to a play (*gāndharva* music). *Gāndharva* was a term derived from the word *gandharva* and associated with the idea of 'deities delighting in music'.

Five other types of *gītis* are mentioned, notably by Mataṅga and Śārṅgadeva; Mataṅga's earlier text mentions seven *gītis* which, he says, have been accepted by Bharata and other ancient musicologists as *gīti* with different forms, but later texts describe five.[5] In general, *gītis* are melodic phenomena which comprise melodic movements (*varṇas*), ornamentations (*alaṅkāras*), syllables (text) and tempo. Consequently there are three aspects to *gītis* – text, rhythm and tones. The five categories are described as follows. There are the *gītis* which refer to style or aesthetic models and which can be distinguished on the basis of their tones (*svara*), how the tones are rendered; scalar interpretation is secondary to this. In *Śuddha gīti,* 'pure', the tones are said to be soft, following a straight and simple path. Mysterious though it may seem, masters of this style can present a whole *rāga* by the utterance of a single tone. This, of course, raises a question about the capacity of listening to such renditions. In *Bhinnā gīti*, described as 'deviant', the tones are described as fast, not straight in sequence and embellished with ornaments giving this style a distinctive quality. *Gauḍī gīti* is said to have a variety of attributes which refer both to an area of eastern India as well as to an elaborate style of prose literature. It is of a serious nature, using special ornaments in all three registers.[6] The musical appeal of *Vesarā gīti* is a combination of its charm and speed. *Sādhāraṇī gīti* is a mixture of the previous four styles. Some of these characteristics have been retained and can be heard in the introductory *ālāpa* rendered by certain *dhrupada* singers.

The five groups are used as a system for allocating the thirty *grāma rāgas* and it seems that in the *grāma rāga* system, style (*gīti*) was the most important criterion for grouping *rāgas* together. According to this system, distinction between *rāgas* in different styles (*gītis*) could be made on the basis of ornamentation. The first category, *śuddha gīti*, includes five of the seven primary *grāma rāgas*. The remaining two were *sa-grāma and ma-grāma* referred to in Chapter 5.

As with other themes in this book the interest lies not only in the subject matter itself but in the extent to which musical ideas and practice have survived and still exist in contemporary performance. *Dhrupada*, the most ancient of northern India's vocal classical musical traditions, has, it seems, inherited both the syllable-rhythm form and well as the tone form of *gīti*. The five *gītis* appear to contain the seeds of the various schools of music (*bānīs*) in *dhrupada* although they were not equivalent. These schools of music are referred to as: *śuddha*, *gobarhāra*, *khaṇḍāra*, *ḍāgara* and *nauhāra*, and, when *dhrupada* was flourishing, each had its distinctive quality, influenced, it would seem, by those stylistic features which lent musical appeal. The exact correspondence between the schools of music (*bānī*) and style (*gīti*) is not clear and consequently different theories have arisen about this.[7] They describe different ways of rendering the tones and there is no doubt about this influence. In fact, such is their importance, that they should take precedence over scalar interpretations of *rāgas* in the initial stages of learning, for, as with language, there are certain things which cannot be conveyed by the written word but can only be passed on by the teacher through tradition. The particular way of rendering tones (*svaras*) in *rāgas* has to be passed on by means of osmosis through the relationship which exists in the disciple/teacher/tradition (*guru-śiṣya-parampara*).[8] Now the system of *bānīs* has, to a large extent, been lost, though there are singers who still maintain fragments of some of them. The strongest of these *bānīs,* at the present time, is the *ḍāgar* style of *dhrupada.*

Two terms which are heard in association with one another are *gāndharva* and *gāna*. *Gāndharva* in a broad sense referred to all music, but in a specific sense it constituted a corpus of music regulated by strictly defined rules. Certain chapters of the *Nāṭya Śāstra* deal with this subject, as does the *Dattilam*, a small work sometimes said to be closely connected with that of Bharata. As formalized music it was the genre of ritual music performed during the prelude to a play. *Gīti* in this context, as has been said before, was a technical term relating to certain characteristic renderings of syllables and words in a song. *Gāna*, on the other hand, was the genre of incidental music used for the ancient theatre. *Gāna* included regional forms of music which did not follow the rules of *gāndharva* music which has been categorized as the music of *mārga* ('the path'). In other words, *gāna* were the dramatic songs, the *dhruvā*, performed during the play itself. There were 64 kinds of *gāna* or *dhruvā* and these have been described in the *Nāṭya Śāstra.*[9] In this same work *gāna* is also the name given to 18 forms of *jāti*, pure and mixed; the *Rāmāyaṇa*, for example, refers to 7 pure *jātigānas* and 11 mixed *jātigānas*. (Canon

IV). Although it has been said that both the *gītis* and the *gānas* have their roots in the *grāmas*, *ṣaḍja* and *madhyama*, it is more likely that the term *gīti* refers to very old forms of song whose antiquity may be as old as the *grāmas* themselves.

A characteristic of some contemporary musical styles is the repetition of syllables or words and even juggling with syllables for the sake of rhythmic and melodic improvisation. This can be heard, for example, in *khayāl* and notably in the Ḍāgar style of *dhrupada* during the *laykārī* part of the performance.[10] Patterns of syllabic formations in the text/rhythm form of *gīti* have already been mentioned and repetition of a phrase or a word was quite usual in *gāndharva*. In *gāndharva* two words could be sung one after another and split syllabically in such a way as to render the meaning unintelligible but provide interesting improvisational possibilities. This is quite common in contemporary classical singing too. Sometimes it is simply prolongation of one syllable which leads to the distortion. For example, '*raaja aaye*' (the king came) could easily become '*raa jaiye*' if the first syllable is sustained. Bharata also describes the use of apparently meaningless syllables which he ascribes to Brahmā, naming them *nirgīta* and *bahirgīta*.[11] The drama, as recounted by Bharata, began with an invocation to focus the audience and to create an atmosphere and this is where such syllables were used. Abhināva's later commentary on this says that only certain syllables were used for the attainment of 'unseen results' or spiritual benefit, a practice in use since time immemorial, because they were on a level with Vedic *mantras*.[12] This practice, the use of syllables with melody, is an important feature of the three *ālāpa* stages of a *dhrupada* recitation and because of their acclaimed mantric derivation, necessitates a reverential approach.[13]

From references given in Pāṇini's grammatical work[14] compiled around 600 BC, and from carvings on stone pillars, one comes to understand that music was a special part of life at that time. Various *sūtras* refer to music-making during this period of history. Stories were sung rather like ballads and accompanied by the *vīṇā*. Songs sung without this accompaniment were considered inferior songs.[15] The *vīṇā* appears to have been played in two ways, with or without a plectrum, but the *vīṇā* as an independent instrument came later. After the rise of Buddhism (500-350 BC) the moral stories surrounding the life of Buddha, known as the *jātaka* stories, were full of music. Moreover, details of the music at that time were recorded on *stūpas* (domed buildings erected as Bhuddist shrines), an indication that music must have been very popular for it to have been engraved in this way, and that this music was for all.[16] During the time of the *Rāmāyaṇa* (200 BC to AD 200) dance, instrumental music and song were popular in all cities with a flourishing cultural life such as Ayodhya. There were professional singers who sang ballads and the singing of the *Rāmāyaṇa* was considered to be a current form of *mārga saṅgīta*.[17] Thus music flourished throughout the ancient history of Northern India. There is considerably more that can be said about the practice of music during these early years but a brief glimpse has to suffice for the purposes of this book.

Another early musical form which has exerted an influence on the present state of performance practice is *kīrtana*. The word *kīrtana* comes from the Sanskrit root '*kīrt*' which means, 'to mention, tell, name, recite, repeat, relate, declare, communicate, commemorate, celebrate, praise, glorify'.[18] Consequently it has come to mean 'singing the praises of God'. Historically, this was a devotional music performed in the temples as a component of *bhakti* (adoration or devotion). It is supposed to have its origins in the Vedas, as, alongside 'knowledge' and 'action', the Veda also describes '*bhakti*'. It is also supposed that the beginnings of *kīrtana* lie in the early chants of Buddhists. It is possible, too, that *kīrtana* derived some of its grammar from early song forms whose melodic and rhythmic structures were quite specific, not allowing for improvisation. Since these early beginnings, *kīrtana* is well known as a component of *bhakti* all over India, and different regions of the country have had one great devotee or the other as the originator of a particular form of *kīrtana*. The mystic experience of *bhakti* (adoration) has been a potent force behind Indian culture. It is generally accepted that the early Vaishnavaite philosophy and religion gave an immense impetus to the *bhakti* feeling wherein the Godhead is the Adored, just as in the Sufi tradition the Godhead is referred to as the Friend or Beloved. In Bengal, for example, *kīrtana* became a form of community hymn-singing which was introduced at the time of Chaitanya Mahaprabhu (1486-1533) in connection with a *bhakti* revival; it is sometimes referred to as *pada gāna*. This type of *kīrtana* is based on parts of the *Kṛṣṇa* legend, describing the mystic love of *Kṛṣṇa* and *Rādha*. As a form of sung prayer, singing of the Name, it was carried to remote villages and in this way worship took on a particular social aspect, the presentation of philosophy in the form of songs having a special attraction.

A verse in a treatise called the *Śrīmadbhāgavata Māhātmya* (VI. 86,87), described as a late *Purāṇa* and therefore thought to have been written around AD 1000, gives a clear description of how *kīrtana* was to be performed. As V.R. Ratate reports in the 1990 edition of the Dhrupad Annual it describes keeping rhythm by means of small cymbals and large bronze cymbals, playing the *vīṇā* (a long-necked, lute-like instrument), singing, playing the *mṛdaṅga* (a double-headed, cylindrical drum) and four princes singing '*Jaya Jaya*' (the meaning is derived from the Sanskrit root *ji* meaning 'to go ahead', 'to conquer'). Not only are there instruments, but someone is there to tell the story or give a discourse and, in the middle, dance the triad of adoration (*bhakti*), knowledge (*jñāna*) and renunciation (*vairāgya*). This, it is said, was the divine assembly of *kīrtana* which delighted the Lord. It is even possible that some traditions of *kīrtana* are connected with the evolution of Northern India's oldest classical vocal form, *dhrupada*. In the course of time, as with other ancient musical practices in India, the rigours of the tradition of *kīrtana* changed, so that the *vīṇā* and double-headed drum have been replaced by the harmonium and *tabla* in many regions.

Figure 6.1 *Gandharva* musicians, tenth-century sculpture, Northern India

A discussion of the history of musical forms has to include *prabandha*. It is a term frequently mentioned, though complex to describe and obscure in origin. Having become the generic term for the independent art songs of mediaeval India, it is associated with the period of the thirteenth and fourteenth centuries. The meaning of the word indicates something that is 'well-bound', but its interpretation in terms of musical practice is likely to have changed considerably over time. Indeed, one stream of theoretical speculation describes *dhruva*, meaning that which is fixed and steady, and its associated word *pada*, meaning poetry or verse, as having derived from the recitation of *Sāma Veda*. This form of song developed into other vocal styles known as *chandha* and *prabandha* with the use of metre and verse. *Prabandha* songs subsequently divided into four parts known as *sthāyī, antarā, sañchārī* and *ābhoga.* But the first indications of a type of musical *prabandha* are to be found in Bharata's *Nāṭya Śāstra.* Here, abut 64 *dhruvā-prabandhas* are mentioned in the context of the dramatic plays, the earliest recorded information about secular song. Again there is the sense of different streams of musical influence coming together. A later but nevertheless early reference is to be found in the final canto of Mataṅga's eighth-century work, the *Bṛhaddeśī,* but by the time of Śārṇgadeva's revered work during the thirteenth century Mataṅga's limited number of *prabandhas* have increased considerably. Moreover he differs from Śārṇgadeva who included the *dhruvā-prabandhas* as sacred music (*gāndharva*) being different from regional songs (*deśī*). Because *prabandha* was an expanding concept the need for categorization became necessary but the distinctions between the various types are often unclear. By the seventeenth century the term was no longer in use, though some of its characteristic musical features have remained within the tradition of art song in India. In general, the *prabandha* which was sung in Sanskrit was the precursor of *dhrupada,* but before *prabandha* there were different forms of composed song dating back to the Vedic period.

Such is the capacity of Indian theorists for division and subdivision that the 'bound' form of *prabandha* has again three forms, *prabandha, vastu* – indicating structure – and *rūpaka* (of good form). Śārṅgadeva talks of four parts of a *prabandha* and six limbs or aspects (*aṅga*) relating to text and rhythm. Moreover, *prabandha* relates to five *jātis* (species), each *jāti* having a different number of aspects attributed to it.[19] As we do not consider a detailed account of all the categories of differentiation of *prabandha* to be relevant to this book and as the subject has been explored by other writers on the subject, only a brief outline indicating the complexity of the subject will be given here.[20] Broadly speaking it can be said that the *prabandhas* are of two types: ' bound or regulated' (*nibaddha*) and 'not bound' (*anibaddha*). It has been suggested that the 'bound' form was a precursor of *kīrtana,*[21] whereas the 'unbound' form consisted of musical sections (*dhātus*) and their components (*aṅgas*). While the latter is not *ālāpa,* as is sometimes maintained, sections of *ālāpa* may be included in a *prabandha.*[22] The bound or restricted form of *prabandha,* on the other hand, refers to the song. From this description of the two forms it is possible to understand the connection with current performance practice in *dhrupada* rendition. Indeed, it is believed today that *dhrupada* was born out of a category of *prabandha* referred to by Śārṅgadeva in the thirteenth-century as *Sālaga Sūdda Prabandha,* which in turn was born out of earlier varieties of *prabandha.* However, agreement over this is by no means unanimous. For a musical genre is not just a question of inherited structural forms but is as much to do with establishing stylistic features and passing them on through tradition.

Vikṛtis

An important and significant feature of Vedic recitation is that it makes use of a method of word division with repetition and patterning. The act of preservation of Vedic texts, in the absence of a written form of notation, has already been mentioned in Chapter 4. The Vedic texts were transmitted orally, by word of mouth, from father to son, from master to disciple. It was, and still is, a method of transmission which both depended upon and strengthened the human capacity for memory. Essentially the Vedas, also referred to as *śruti* (that which is heard), consisted of knowledge which was in the realm of memory rather than in the realm of written scripture. For this reason, recitation was a crucial factor in preservation. There are, of course, other reasons why recitation is important and these have already been alluded to in previous chapters. Here we focus mainly on recitation as a method of preservation.

The starting point is that the same text can be presented in different ways or patterns. There are three basic forms (*vikṛtis*) from which a further eight forms are derived. The three basic forms are *saṁhitā*, where phonetic changes (*sandhi*) have been introduced at the point where words join together, *pada pāṭhaḥ*, where the words of the text are separate, and *krama pāṭhaḥ*, where the words of the text progress in pairs, 'by step'. *Saṁhitā* reproduces the words of the text as a cohesive string of sounds which is conducive to a certain flow of energy. From a practical point of view *pada pāṭhaḥ* clarifies any ambiguity in meaning which may arise when there is more than one possibility for dividing the words of a text which is in the *saṁhita* form. The separation between the words inevitably introduces slight pauses, which changes the energy within the *mantra*. In *krama pāṭhaḥ*, where the words are paired, there is both the use of *sandhi* where words within the pair are joined, as well as pauses between the pairs of words. The particle *iti*, meaning 'thus' or 'in this manner', is introduced at specific points of pause, at the end of a phrase, as the examples below show. This arrangement again changes the system of energy within the text.

As has been mentioned in Chapter 3, the Vedas deal with the mechanics of the many levels of existence, and consequently with man's connection and resonance with intelligences and energies in this hierarchy. It is not surprising therefore that the *Yājñavalkya Śikṣā*, for example, associates *saṁhitā* with the sun and its related subtle energies, *pada pāṭhaḥ* with the moon and the ancestors, and *krama pāṭhaḥ* with a subtle world beyond the sun and the moon.[23] These forms of recitation are also represented by the names of three sacred Indian rivers, the *Ganges*, *Yamunā* and *Saraswatī*. They in turn represent the three currents of energy within the human body referred to as *iḍā*, *piṅgalā* and *suṣumnā*.[24] Outer references indicate an inner meaning; these are the currents of energy which flow along the seven *cakras*. As has been said before, although there is no specific reference to *cakras* in the Vedas, their understanding is conveyed within the language of the texts. Not only do these three forms of recitation relate to inner experience, they can also affect the way in which specific consonants, if pronounced correctly, will resonate. The proper pronunciation of consonants in the context where they occur may be essential. For example, the consonant '*ha*' will resonate in the heart centre in *saṁhitā* recitation and in the throat centre in *pada pāṭhaḥ* recitation.[25] Thus, it is said, Vedic ritual should be performed on the shores of the river of knowledge and consciousness, an image which reflects both a metaphorical and literal meaning.

Here is an example used to demonstrate the different forms of recitation in the *Ṛg Veda,* 'In Praise of Herbs'.[26] This translates as:

> With the soma plant as their Sovereign Lord, the plants converse together saying, 'O King, we help that one to whom the remedy is given by a Brāhman.'

Saṁhitā pāṭhaḥ

oṣadhayaḥ saṁvadantesomenasaharajñā ।

yasmaikṛnotibrāhmaṇastaṁ rājan pārayāmasi ॥

Pada pāṭhaḥ

Word progression: 1 2 3 4 5 6 7 8 9 10 11 12

oṣadhayaḥ । saṁ । vadante । somena । saha । rājñā

1 2 3 4 5 6

yasmai । kṛṇoti । brāmaṇaḥ । taṁ । rājan । pārayāmasi ॥

7 8 9 10 11 12

Krama pāṭhaḥ

Word progression: 12 23 34 45 56 iti 6
78 89 910 1011 1112 12 iti 12 ॥

oṣadhayaḥ saṁ । saṁ vadante । vadante somena । somena saha । saha rājñā ।

1 2 2 3 3 4 4 5 5 6

rājñeti rājñā

6 iti 6

yasmai kṛṇoti I kṛṇoti brāhmaṇaḥ I brāhmaṇastaṁ I taṁ rājan I rājan

7 8 8 9 9 10 10 11 11

pārayāmasi I pārayāmasiti pārayāmasi II

12 12 iti 12

The way in which the text is to be varied through the use of different formulae or patterns of words and how the resulting words or syllables are to be accented depends on the particular tradition of recitation.[27] There are traditionally eight forms or patterns (*aṣṭa vikṛti*) which are known as: *jaṭā* (braid or plait), *daṇda* (staff), *mālā* (garland), *rekhā* (row), *dhvaja* (flag), *ghana* (dense or bell), *ratha* (chariot) and *śikhā* (topknot). In all the *vikṛtis* two words must be used at a time and the pattern is made up from these. There are further complexities which could be added to the discussion.

The first *vikṛti* or variation is *jaṭā*. *Jaṭā* means 'braid' and the words of the verse, taken two at a time, are braided or plaited as follows:

Word progression:	12	21	12
	23	32	23
	34	43	34
	45	54	45
	56	65	56
	6 iti 6		

The appropriate laws of *sandhi* are observed where words meet, so that the arrangement is as follows:

oṣadhayas saṁ samoṣadhaya oṣadhayas sam II

1 2 2 1 1 2

saṁ vadante vadante saṁ saṁ vadante II

2 3 3 2 2 3

vadante somena somena vadante vadante somena II

3 4 4 3 3 4

somena saha saha somena somena saha II

4 5 5 4 4 5

saha rājñā, rājñā saha saha rājñā ||

5 6 5 6 5 6

rājñeti rājñā ||

6 iti 6

Daṇḍaḥ

Word progression:

12	21				
12	23	321			
12	23	34	4321		
12	23	34	45	54321	
12	23	34	45	56	654321
12	23	34	45	56	6 iti 6

oṣadhayaḥ saṁ || samoṣadhayaḥ |

oṣadhayaḥ saṁ | saṁ vadante || vadante samoṣadhayaḥ |

oṣadhayaḥ saṁ | saṁ vadante | vadante somena || somena vadante

samoṣadhayaḥ |

oṣadhayaḥ saṁ | saṁ vadante | vadante somena || somena saha ||

saha somena vadante samoṣadhayaḥ |

oṣadhayaḥ saṁ | saṁ vadante | vadante somena || somena saha | saha rājñā ||

rājñā saha somena vadante samoṣadhayaḥ |

oṣadhayaḥ saṁ | saṁ vadante | vadante somena || somena saha | saha rājñā ||

rājñeti rājñā |

There are young Ṛg Vedins in Vārāṇasī who are taught that, of the eight *vkṛtis*, *jaṭā* and *daṇḍaḥ* are important because it is from these two that the others are derived. For example, *jaṭā* gives rise to *puṣpamālā* and *śikhā*, whereas *rekhā*, *dhvaja* and *rathā* are derived from *daṇḍaḥ*. *Ghaṇa*, on the other hand, is derived from both *jaṭā* and *daṇḍaḥ*.

Puṣpamālā (garland of flowers) is a formula where no *sandhi* is used and *iti* comes at the end of each line. It is said that the words are pierced just like the flowers of a garland in the making:

Word progression:	12	21	12	iti	
	23	32	23	iti	
	34	43	34	iti	and so on

Rekhā

Word progression:	12	21	12
	234	432	23
	3456	6543	34
	4556	6 iti 6	

oṣádhayaḥ saṁ samoṣádhayaḥ oṣádhayaḥ saṁ ॥

saṁ vádante somena । somena vadante saṁ । saṁ vádante ॥

vadante somena saha rājñā । rājñā saha somena vadante । vadante somena ॥

somena saha saha rājñā । rājñeti rājñā ॥

Ghaṇaḥ

This example of the *ghaṇa* (dense) formula or pattern gives a glimpse of how complex the system can become. Both the *Ṛg Veda* and *Yajur Veda,* Mādhyandina Branch, make use of this formula arranged as follows:

Word progression:	1221	123	321	123	
	2332	234	432	234	and so on

oṣádhayaḥ saṁ samoṣádhaya oṣádhayaḥ saṁ vádante vadante samoṣádhaya

1 2 2 1 1 2 3 3 2 1

oṣádhayaḥ saṁ vádante ॥

1 2 3

saṁ vádante vadante saṁ saṁ vádante soména soména vadante saṁ

2 3 3 2 2 3 4 4 3 2

saṁ vádante soména ||

2 3 4 and so on.

Initiation into these various forms of recitation begins early in a child's life, around six to eight years, when the memory absorbs the process most easily. It is said by some that the first three forms of recitation are the oldest, but, as has been observed before, it is almost impossible to date chronologically that which has been preserved by means of an oral tradition. It is a system which is likely to be more durable than many other forms of written preservation of material which does not survive the passage of time. *Sāma Veda* is not recited by these methods but is chanted, although, again, both text and melody forms are heard and memorized. An important point of interest is the way in which both of these ancient systems have influenced contemporary performance practice. Let each word represent a tone and immediately there is a system of patterning which can be heard exploited in instrumental performance. When the technique of combining melodic fragments is used, referred to in the west as centonization, we can detect a procedure which has influenced *rāga* exposition as it is heard today as well as other non-Indian forms of music.

If the system of Indian music is considered as a whole, it is clear that there are two main streams. There is music which is of the nature of free melody, not composed (*anibaddha*), and there are songs which are composed (*nibaddha*). These two aspects of Indian classical music, or streams of influence, have been present for thousands of years.

Finally, however, neither form nor style have meaning without that quality which the Indian tradition describes as *svara sādhanā*, a technique resulting from disciplined practice of tones. It is not easy work because it requires solitary work on the tones of the musical scale, but it is the means whereby a particular element or subtle quality can enter the singing voice and allow devotion (*bhakti*) to shine through. It is said by some that the power of the tones is the secret of singing because this '*svara*' is a quality which hides within the musical tone. For sacred music or singing the praises of God has two aspects: the outer and the inner. The outer side is the arrangement of words and tones, the inner side is the mysterious process whereby the wandering mind is stabilized and a vista of inner consciousness is opened bringing joy and peace.

Notes

1 Khan, 1977, p. 19.
2 Singh, 1995, p. 2.
3 Shringy, and Sharma, 1991 p. 10.
4 Lath, p. 425.
5 Sharma, 2000, p. 246.
6 *Ohāṭi* is a technique of producing soft tones in the lower register embellished with *kampita gamaka* – a type of specifically applied vibrato. In order to achieve the correct effect the head has to be bent forward so as to touch the chest with the chin. Tones embellished in this way may be sung in all three registers.
7 Indurama Srivastava (1980), *Dhrupada*, Motilal Banarsidass Publishers Pvt. Ltd, Delhi, p. 49.
8 Dr Ritwik Sanyal, Banāras Hindu University, personal communication 1998.
9 Bharata, *Nāṭya Śāstra*, 32.
10 R. Sanyal and D.R. Widdess (1994), 'Some Techniques of Layakārī in the Ḍāgar Tradition', *Dhrupad Annual*, All India Kashi Raj Trust, Vārāṇasī, vol. IX p. 19.
11 Bharata, *Nāṭya Śāstra* 31-45a; the section describing *Pūrvaraṅga*, the prelude to the play itself.
12 Abhinavagupta, a great philosopher and musicologist of the tenth-century AD, who commented on the entire *Nāṭya Śāstra*.
13 The *mantra* from which the syllables, sometimes referred to as *nom-tom* syllables, used in *dhrupada ālāpa*, are said to be derived, is: *'Om Hari Nārāyaṇa, taraṇa, tārana avanti Hari Om'*. In the Ḍāgar *dhrupada* tradition, where syllables are used exclusively during the *ālāpa* sections, it is said that *Om* is replaced by the syllable *num*, *Hari* is represented by *ri*, and *ra* stands for *Nārāyaṇa*. This interpretation may not be accepted by all who practise *dhrupada*.
14 The *Aṣṭādhyāyī* of Pāṇini.
15 Singh, 1994, p. 224.
16 Singh, 1994, p. 231.
17 Singh, 1994, p. 158.
18 Monier-Williams, p. 285.
19 Prajñānānanda, p. 179.
20 For more detailed descriptions of the history of *prabandha* the reader is referred to Rowell, 1992; Widdess, 1994; and Prajñānānanda, 1973.
21 Premalatha, p. 220.
22 Widdess, 1994, p. 404.
23 *Yājñavalkya Śikṣā*, 1:32.
24 *Yājñavalkya Śikṣā*, 1:33.
25 *Yājñavalkya Śikṣā*, 2:57.
26 *Ṛg Veda*, Part 10, *sūkta* (hymn) 97, *mantra* 22.
27 See Chapter 3.

Chapter 7
Style

What do we see as the principal expression of life in the beauty visible before us? It is movement. In line, in colour, in the changes of the seasons, in the rising and falling of the waves, in the wind, in the storm, in all the beauty of nature there is constant movement.[1]

So it is in music too. Style, the method or the manner of performance, is the mode of expression for this beauty. However, these are aspects of musical rendition which frequently elude clear explanation even though, in the case of North Indian music, as well as other musical genres, they constitute its very texture. Some would say that it is in the manner of going, the way of moving from tone to tone that constitutes the very soul of the music, that transforms the bare tones into living organisms. The difficulty lies in trying to describe a melodic microstructure, whose elements of rendition may range from something as obvious as an 'ornament' to those movements within the melodic line which are so transient, so fleeting as to be on the periphery of conscious hearing. It is in this domain, where the nervous system and the subtle body are affected, that the emotions can be stimulated in a subtle and poignant way.[2] It is also the difference between the Western mind and the Indian; the inseparability of content and its expression. Some of the causes of this difference in conceptual thinking may lie in the realm of language, the Sanskrit language. This is a language capable of conveying widened concepts made up of unities of ideas, a process which can be heard reflected in music as the discussion on *alaṅkāra* shows. Many Indian art forms, when they are true to tradition, are to a certain degree a method whereby the participant may ascend from the physical level of vision or hearing to a different dimension of experience.

Who qualifies to render this music? Nārada's early work sets out clearly both the required qualities of someone who sings or recites *mantras* and the defects which will prevent this.[3] The *Yājñavalkya Śikṣā* similarly describes qualities in an individual which will prevent proper recitation of the *mantras*.[4] Indeed, the subject of merits and demerits in Sanskrit treatises (*guṇas* and *doṣas*) is an extensive one.[5] Bharata's early work on dramaturgy and music similarly sets out those aspects of character which the ideal spectator of a drama should possess,[6] a seemingly impossible achievement but, reassuringly, he adds later that all these various qualities would not necessarily reside in one single spectator.[7] The point to note is that the spectator was an important part of a performance. The guidelines for those who qualify primarily as singers, but also as musicians, have been rigorously maintained within the oral tradition and described in painstaking detail in the *śāstric* literature.

From the special qualities of the performer and listener we turn to the particular properties of musical sound. These are the distinctive features of the musical traditions of India. It is reasonable to start an exploration with some of the earliest concepts, such as those which exist in Vedic recitation. In those styles of Vedic recitation which make use of no more than three accents or tones, we have already spoken of the *svarita* accent as not only an intermediary tone in relation to *udātta* and *anudātta* accents (raised and lowered accents) but also as having the effect of a 'grace'.[8] In Sāmavedic recitation, what may be looked upon as simple ornamentation may have formed the basis of more complicated melodic movements and ornamentation of later times; a tone could be lengthened for up to two time measures, tones could be rendered in quick succession, or in quick succession but in reverse order, or there could be a specific order of tones such as one might find in an *alaṅkāra* and other groups of tones which resembled a small *tāna*. The transition from some tones to others was to be undertaken smoothly and without a break, an instruction which seems to anticipate the sense of continuity and fluidity which has since characterized the performance of classical vocal music and is particularly noticeable in the Ḍāgar style of rendering slow *ālāpa*.

The term *gamaka* is a very accommodative term in Indian music terminology. Etymologically the word stems from the Sanskrit root '*gam*' meaning 'to go' and from this origin it encompasses a variety of tonal movements. The definition implies 'causing to understand', 'making clear or intelligible', 'explanatory', 'leading to clearness'.[9] It is not found in the early work attributed to Bharata, the *Nāṭya Śāstra*, but *kampa* is mentioned, meaning a shake or a quiver, or perhaps a touch of vibrato on a specified tone.[10] It is possible that it derived from the *svarita* accent of Vedic recitation because, although its vibratory status is not made clear, the term *kampa* appears in the *Nāradīya Śikṣā*.[11] The Nambudirī *Jaiminīyas* have a distinctive style of recitation using *kampa* extensively in their chants. However, it is difficult to say whether this is due to their being an old Sāmavedic tradition or to some other reason, such as a regional characteristic. Much later, in mediaeval treatises, *kampana* continues to refer to a tone which is 'shaken', but subsequently it has acquired a meaning closer to the Western term vibrato. It should be noted, however:

> ... that the vibrato itself is present in Indian music as a conscious form element in the grace called the *kampana* (shake). This is a consciously used embellishment akin to the vibrato ... There is another grace called the āndolana (swing) which is much slower. What is essential to realize here is that the vibrato is employed *consciously* and *infrequently* in Indian music ... But in the 'lighter' music of the films and 'ham' singers vibrato is common.[12]

Deva's experiments with the presence of vibrato in Indian singers (1981) revealed that their singing did not exhibit this characteristic except in the form of *kampana*. In the classical forms of music the old idea, described by Bharata, has remained.

It is in the work attributed to the sage Nārada that the word *śruti*, implying 'that which is heard', is specifically mentioned in the context of tone quality. The importance of understanding this concept is clearly stressed in this work where it is said that one who does not know the distinction between the *śrutis* is not to be recognized as a teacher.[13] However, when discussing this concept a wary ear is necessary in order to determine whether the term is referring to tonal shades, harmonics, or microtonal intervals. In this *śikṣā* the term *śruti* stands for the particular expression of the tone and not the microtonic intervals between tones that constitute the octave.[14] This set of *śrutis* were five in number: *dīptā*, having the quality of brightness or intensity, *āyatā*, an extended tone, *karuṇā*, subdued, *mṛdu*, soft, and *madhyama* or moderate. Moreover, three of the five *śrutis* – *dīptā*, *mṛdu* and *karuṇā* – are said to be derived from the three Vedic accents, implying that Vedic recitation was an inspiration for musical development. The implication is that there was scope, at some stage of the development of chant practice, for more subtlety of expression woven into the process of recitation than might at first seem to be the case. The assumption often made is that the ancient *svaras* or tones were treated as fixed pitches at specific intervals of the octave, a supposition derived from the way in which they were first described in the *Nāṭya Śāstra*. In practice, tones were very likely to have been adjusted by ear at the time of performance and there may have been considerable variation in intonation, just as there is today. We may also wonder whether there were aspects of voice culture and aesthetics not heard in present-day recitation, a refinement of rendition which has become distorted or lost altogether. One has only to experiment by taking a typical musical phrase from the Sāmavedic repertoire and rendering it in contemporary Ḍāgar *bāni* (school of music) style, or any other style, to hear what the possibilities could have been long ago.

However, the names of the *śrutis* that Nārada mentions are quite different from those mentioned by Bharata and Śārṅgadeva. The scheme of twenty-two *śrutis* mentioned in the *Nāṭya Śāstra* which relates to the positions of the *svaras sa*, *ri*, *ga*, *ma*, *pa*, *dha* and *ni*, on the fourth, seventh, ninth, thirteenth, seventeenth, twentieth and twenty-second *śrutis* respectively, could represent a set of equal intervals as positions in the octave or unequal intervals when expressed as ratios.[15] They determined the intrinsic nature of the *grāma rāgas*. It is reasonable, therefore, to describe both sets of *śrutis* as tonal inflections which gave scope for creating interesting variations in terms of pitch, volume and timbre.

There are many aspects of Indian music whose intrinsic purpose has become largely forgotten. A regeneration of meaning could occur, for example, if one remembered that the seven tones, *ṣaḍja*, *ṛṣabha*, *gāndhāra*, *madhyama*, *pañcama*, *dhaivata* and *niṣāda*, evolve out of the breath or life-force as it comes into contact with different internal parts of the body. In Chapter 2, discussion of the four energies of sound explains how this may come about, but it is the practical application and experience which is important. In singing, the terms are abbreviated and only the first consonant and vowel are used, viz. *sa*, *ri*, *ga*, *ma*, *pa*, *dha*, *ni*, but nevertheless they are still considered to possess special qualities, sometimes described as mantric qualities. There is also a connection with the idea, mentioned in the discussion on *svara sādhanā*, that a single tone in Indian music is a sound which pulsates and has a sense of dimension, a principle which can be heard in some other non-Western musical cultures. The *ney* (end-blown flute) of Mevlevi Sufi music is an example, though there are subtle but distinctive differences in the soundscape which is created thereby.

From the required qualities or *lakṣaṇas* of individuals, mentioned earlier in this chapter, we turn to the *lakṣaṇas* of performance. *Lakṣaṇa* is an old word. It means 'a feature or characteristic, a distinguishing mark'. It is used in the *Nāṭya Śāstra* as is the word *alaṅkāra* which means 'that which makes sufficient'. They are parallel ideas. In poetry, *alaṅkāra* is an embellishment of poetic expression. *Lakṣaṇa* implies something inherent, something which cannot be separated out.[16] Take the human body. Some things are born with the body but other things can be put on such as a ring or bracelet. Bharata described 36 *lakṣaṇas* in the *Nāṭya Śāstra* and only four *alaṅkāra*. Later *alaṅkāra* increased and *lakṣaṇas* decreased so that by the twelfth century the term was almost lost. What later became known as tonal movements of various kinds (*gamaka)* were earlier known as tonal finesses (*svara lakṣaṇas*), implying that a tone has some inherent and inseparable characteristic. This much quoted image from the *Nāṭya Śāstra* gives the idea:

> Like the night without the moon, the river without water,
> The creeper without blossom,
> Like the maiden without adornments is the song without embellishments.[17]

We may even extend the metaphor to other realms and refer to the mind adorned by learning, a concept which echoes the overall idea that *gamaka* (tonal movements) are those aspects of the music which make the original structure 'intelligible'. Although originally *alaṅkāra* referred to the manner of tone production, or what is now referred to as voice culture, it later came to mean motif.[18] By the time of the *Saṅgīta Ratnākara*, compiled by Śārṅgadeva around the thirteenth century, *alaṅkāra* had come to mean a specific pattern of tones. This pattern of tones was described as a component of melodic movement (*varṇa*), that melodic movement which makes the structure of the music.[19] They were melodic flourishes which lent colour and charm to these melodic movements.[20] Discrimination was the key to aesthetic appeal, as it should be today:

> Melody should be embellished by these (ornamentations) without disrupting the tone-pattern (*varṇa*), for ornaments are to be put on properly so that the girdle is not tied to the breast.[21]

In other words, ornaments are to be applied in the right place. For example, ornamentation which is appropriate to the vocal styles of *ṭhumri* and *khayāl* would be inappropriate in a performance of *dhrupada*. The Ḍāgar genre of *dhrupada* singing has ten specific *svara lakṣaṇas* or tonal finesses. To illustrate what this means they are listed as follows:

ākār	A way of rendering a tone which conveys a sense of a tonal zone rather than a dimensionless pitch. The process begins around the tone *Sa*, the tonic.
ḍagar	The pathway which shows typical phrases of the *rāga*.
dhuran	The singer expounds the tones, together with *śrutis*, in rounded and ascending order.
muran	Round melodic patterns of tones in a descending direction.
kampita	A rapid movement between a substantive tone and its neighbour, a small oscillation or 'shake'. For example, *sa ni sa ni*.
āndolita	A slower, smoother oscillation between two adjacent tones within a *rāga*.
lahaka	The Ḍāgar style uses breath force to make tones move in a lashing manner, a long, swiftly moving glissando from an unspecified lower pitch. *Hukara* is where singing is intoned with the mouth closed, as for the syllable '*num*'.
gamaka	Successive tones, uttered using the Ḍāgar system of mantric syllables, are repeatedly stressed.
huḍaka	Articulation is heavy and the tones are pulled upwards using extra breath force. This creates a humming sound.
sphūrti	The tones are rendered in very fast tempo, with different rhythmic variations, giving a 'flashing' effect. This *lakṣaṇa* is used in the *jhālā* portion of the *ālāpa*.

It is in an eighth-century work by Mataṅga that the technique of note permutation (*svara prastāra*) is clearly described. This concept, also called *prastāra alaṅkāra*, consists of progressing and extending the melodic range tone by tone. Ascending and descending patterns using two, three, four, five, six or seven tones are used. In the same work other patterns of tone sequences occur;

four-tone patterns, for example, were referred to as *kūṭa tānas*.[22] Interestingly, the speed at which such small patterns are rendered is crucial to their role as an embellishment or as something else. At a very fast speed they may be perceived as a decorative adjunct to a substantive tone, referred to in Baroque improvisation as diminutions. At a slower speed, the same combination of tones may be perceived as scalar material within the melodic contour. Thus, there were *alaṅkāra* which related to tonal sequences and *alaṅkāra* which were related to qualities of intonation; they were melody-orientated or tone-orientated.

While the distinction between *lakṣaṇa* and *alaṅkāra* was an overlapping and evolving one, so too was the differentiation between *alaṅkāra* and *gamaka*. It was not until the thirteenth century, in Śārṅgadeva's *Saṅgīta Ratnākara*, that these two concepts were separated out. Here are two definitions of *gamaka* which convey the idea:

> In a melodic structure, the formulation of a tonal shade arising out of a *svara's* own *śruti* and resorting to that of another *śruti* is demonstrated to be *gamaka*.[23]

> The shaking of tone that is delightful to the listener's mind is (called) *gamaka*.[24]

These descriptions have been reformulated in recent times, notably by B.C. Deva whose definition is often quoted:

> When, in music, a tone moves from its own pitch towards another so that the second sound passes like a shadow over it, this is called *gamaka*.[25]

Thus, *gamaka* in musical treatises includes all types of pitch variation, tonal nuances, varying voice productions, subtleties of dynamics and time. Somewhat confusingly, in contemporary parlance it is often used synonymously with *alaṅkāra* as a term for ornamentation or embellishment, for the original term, *alaṅkāra*, was never abolished in Indian music. It reflects a situation inherited from the past when the concepts of *varṇa* (melodic contour) and *alaṅkāra* included the idea of *gamaka*.

The newcomer to Indian music, confronted by a seemingly incomprehensible world of sound-shapes, melodic wanderings, whorls of incandescent sounds, a myriad intricate weavings of melodic fragments which are somehow made to coalesce into a single overriding and even overwhelming sound-impression, may well wonder at such definitions. For every Indian oral tradition has a system of *gamakas* or *svara lakṣaṇas* as an essential part of a system of improvisation. One may take, as one example, the system of tonal rendition (*ākāra*) used during the initial slow *ālāpa* stage of a *dhrupada* performance. Here one may hear both ascending and descending progressions which sometimes use a technique analogous to spiralling. Creation is full of spirals; they take place around a still point.

If the written tradition of music is taken into consideration, the reader, if he or she is not bored or confused by so much technical detail, cannot fail to be impressed by the fine levels of sound discrimination which musicologists in the past observed and tried to describe. Just as perceived and spoken sound in the form of 'the word' was such a serious subject of study by ancient philosophers and phoneticians, so too did the tradition of musicology reflect a minutiae of analysis in 'hair's-breadth' detail of differences between sounds and the transitive elements between substantive tones. Indeed, as long ago as Bharata's early work, it was understood that there were at least three tonal shades of the third and seventh scale degrees. More recently, there are members of the Ḍāgar style of *dhrupada* recitation who say that there are potentially seven shades of any tone in a *rāga*. But why is such detail important? Because therein lies a realm of delicate connections, the aesthetic content of the music, where feelings and subtle emotions can be influenced.

> We must revise our attitude towards ornamentation [*gamaka*]. Ornaments [*gamaka*] are of the essence of music. Indeed, since music is architectonic, it is possible to consider even the largest sections of a composition as being essentially ornamental ... Ornaments [*gamaka*], then, must be considered as inseparable from the structural tones and basic plan which they ornament and to which they give meaning. They themselves are likewise inseparable from and meaningless without the basic substantive tones ... which they ornament.[26]

As for *alaṅkāra*, the numbers of *gamaka* have been listed variously in the musical treatises. The list given by Śārṅgadeva is the one which has often been quoted. It is not proposed to reiterate it here but simply to refer the reader to other sources.[27] As many as 70 *alaṅkāra* are described by Śārṅgadeva whereas previously Dattila considered only 13 as important.[28] The potential for proliferation as well as creative expansion in this dimension of music is obvious. Historically, though, the indication is that the *gāndharva* tradition of music, which was in existence from around 600 BC and considered a sacred form of music, was less ornate than subsequent styles.[29] We may also observe that as different styles of singing, such as Vedic recitation, folk music and devotional music, evolved during the course of time, resulting styles such as *dhrupada*, *khayāl*, *ṭhumrī*, *ghazals* and *bhajans*, have shown the development of a great variety of ways of modulating tones.

As far as theory is concerned, it should be remembered that it is based on the observation of current practice and is not primarily the instigator of practice. Nevertheless, it is worth extending the range of our appreciation of *gamaka*, this pervasive and essential aspect of musical rendition, a little further. Although some of the *gamakas* used in current practice appear to be similar, such as an oscillation on a particular tone, they nevertheless differ from the point of view of their duration, speed, magnitude and manner of production. This difference depends upon the style, the artist and the *rāga* in which they occur.

Although there may be distinctive stylistic characteristics, to arrive at a clear definition of *gamaka* for any particular style is almost impossible. One reason is that vocalists and instrumentalists are not necessarily aware of the *gamakas* they use. This is partly because they arise spontaneously during performance and partly because the oral tradition, where musical learning is imparted from teacher to disciple largely by demonstration and imitation, often does not label what is taught. Although trends may be changing, it certainly used to be true that many vocalists, if you asked them what they were singing, would say, 'I don't know. I just learned it from my *guru*. We did not question what was taught to us.'[30] It is said that quite 50 per cent of the hearing process depends upon memory. This has important implications for the way in which we learn the music of another culture, for not only must we be able to hear the details of a music which we did not grow up with before we can reproduce it, but we must also retrain the memory.

It has been said that the art music of India displays a strong tendency towards surface decoration but to what extent is this true? Take, for example, the *kaṇa svara*, referred to as a device of articulation. As a noun it means 'particle' and as a verb it implies something which 'goes small'. It is a term which has been interpreted variously. In essence it is a very subtle ornament, often no more than a tonal shade, a colour. At its most refined, it operates at the level of inaudible sound, *nāda*, and can only be heard by the trained ear, the inner ear referred to earlier. Such sounds, conceived in the mind but inaudibly uttered, are practised as part of the Ḍāgar style of *dhrupada ālāpa* rendition. At this level, 'ornaments' such as the *kaṇa svara* are no longer operating at the surface of perception. For sound can be distilled, such as one finds in a homoeopathic potency where none of the physical substance remains. On these occasions the materially audible sound has been transcended so that only the essence may be perceived, but, it should be added, usually only by the trained ear, that aspect of the 'ear' which was described in Chapter 2 on the subtleties of pronunciation of mantric Sanskrit in recitation. At its grossest level this feature has been described, using Western terminology, as an appoggiatura and as such has become an ornament, a decorative device. To limit the interpretation of this important characteristic of Indian music is to lose both the subtle artistic and spiritual possibilities of this device and the original understanding which lies in the realm of language.

We should listen again to the music of the great masters of Indian music and we should consider again the levels of ornamentation and embellishment, for the whole is an 'architectonic structure' and within this we may detect the different levels of tonal movement (*gamaka*) and the degrees of aural prominence of the sounds which make up the overall impression of the music. If we apply an aural magnifying glass or microscope to the music we hear at the ordinary level of time, it will become clear that some of what we hear is a compression in time of more substantial melodic material, that there is a process of expansion and contraction at work (as has been suggested in the discussion on *alaṅkāra*). This then constitutes a hierarchy of artistic expression and the need for a corresponding hierarchy of hearing. When this process takes place within the context of the opening slow *ālāpa* of, for example, a *dhrupada* rendition where there is no recognizable rhythm or beat but only the presence of a pulse, both the performer and listener have an opportunity to escape the feeling of musical expectation and experience a different aesthetic or *rasa.* Here, very subtle changes in the nuances of rhythm have the potential to stimulate the relationship between interior and exterior worlds. This is the tradition of esoteric music which is, to a large extent, lost from most cultures. The tendency of the majority of music is exoteric and thus it serves a different purpose.

Indian musicological theory tends to describe the different aesthetic potentialities of musical rendition in terms of the theory of *rasa.* While it is not the purpose of this work to enter too deeply into this complex subject, it should nevertheless be acknowledged as an essential aspect of musical understanding. It is in the *Nātya Śāstra* that this term is first expounded, resulting in an importance which has endured. The literal meaning of *rasa* is 'sap', 'juice' or 'essence' and this is applied to art in the realm of sentiments or emotions. Bharata elaborated the significance of *rasa* in the *Nātya Śāstra,* in terms of categories of emotional experience as well as a catalogue of *rasas* and their corresponding emotional states (*sthāyibhāvas*). Bharata also attempted to link musical structure with emotion, giving tones such as *aṁśa* (predominant note) special functions and emphasis within a particular *jāti* (a melodic progression relating to ancient modes). Thirteen such *rāga* characteristics are listed in the *Saṅgīta Ratnākara.*[31] Realization of the special effect of a tone within a tonal progression was, of course, dependent upon the musician's ability to reveal its particular quality and, in turn, the listener's ability to hear it. In the discussion on *svara sādhanā* special attention is drawn to the importance of disciplined practice of a single tone, but in the context of a musical rendition there are other factors such as graces, tempo and octave level which play a part. For example, *rāgas* where the emphasis is in the upper octave are unlikely to be sombre or particularly dignified in ethos but will reflect a different range of emotions.

Recent writers of the twentieth century have questioned whether the *rasas* described by Bharata are now appropriate, for the work attributed to him was originally a treatise on drama and therefore not wholly applicable to music. During the course of time the range of *rasas* considered to be relevant in music has been reduced. However, the aesthetic purpose of a classical music rendition continues to remain that of trying to transcend any given emotional state indicated by a particular *rāga.* This essential quality is described in the commentary on the *Saṅgīta Ratnākara* by the late Dr Prem Lata Sharma:

> *Rasa* is generally rendered as aesthetic delight, but that does not elucidate the concept adequately. *Rasa* is that delight which is distinguished from pleasure, from sensation and sensual enjoyment in so far as it is to be derived from a state of mind free from the limitations of personal likes and dislikes. *Rasa* is the delight of a consciousness in which emotion is experienced as a universal affection. *Rasa* is not only contemplation but also

a direct experience of beauty and love. The concept of *rasa* is ... 'delight approximating to universal love'.[32]

Included in the concept of *gamaka,* which can give rise to *rasas*, is that of *sthāya,* a complex idea embracing many aspects of musical tone and its embellishments. Ninety-one such musical features are mentioned by Śārṅgadeva. The fact that musicologists accounted for them at this time, in the twelfth and thirteenth centuries, indicates that there must have been a rich and long tradition of such subtleties of musical expression. Indeed, once again, the seeds may be found in Bharata's much earlier work. It is not proposed to give a detailed resumé of this idea here as the reader can refer to the *Saṅgīta Ratnākara* for this. However, we may deduce that, although musical phrases are a characteristic of *Sāma Veda* recitation, it is from this later area of musicology that the importance given to phrases, motifs, musical figures and their embellishments, as compared with the importance attached to scalar concepts, becomes apparent in the literature.[33] In the *Saṅgīta Ratnākara* they fall into four groups. The exquisite details of intonation which musicologists of the time wished to convey can be appreciated by taking just one example. There are, of course, a large number of *sthāyas*, but important among the first group of *sthāyas* listed in the *Saṅgīta Ratnākara*, and described as 'distinct' or 'well-known', is *chāyā*. *Chāyā* means 'shadow', 'reflection', 'image', 'tinge', but it also infers qualities of lustre and beauty and thus conjures up the idea of tonal colour. The analysis becomes even more detailed as six distinct types of this *sthāya* alone are identified.[34]

We may pursue the idea of phrase still further if we agree with Ratanjankar, a twentieth-century writer, when he says that 'phrase is essential to *rāga* expression' – little blocks of tone passages (*svara saṅgatis*) which make up quite 80 per cent of *rāgas*.[35] These small groupings of tones (*svaras*), he says elsewhere, 'are so important that even one and the same scale of *svaras* may give rise to a number of distinct *rāgas* simply by the difference in their treatment as regards emphasis, groupings of tones and little graces of music applied to them'.[36] Indeed, this idea is embedded in the teaching of *rāgas* in the oral tradition of Indian vocal music, as any student blessed with a good teacher can attest to. More important than the ascending and descending scale patterns are the identifying phrases, and in addition to these there are the internal melodic and harmonic relationships, tone to tone, interval to interval and even motif to motif, which characterize a *rāga*.

The underlying importance of phrase has far-reaching and deeper implications, for the idea of continuity within the evolution of North Indian music is intimately bound up with this concept connecting past and present, theory and practice. Sāmavedic recitation and the *śruti* descriptions given by Nārada in the manual attributed to him show how the chants were formed by piecing together components from a repertoire of phrases, a technique referred to as 'centonization'. This ancient 'technique of piecing together melodic fragments to create a musical work undergirds the *rāga* concept of Indian classical music'.[37] However, while the sense of tradition, imbued by tenacity, which underlies the evolution of Indian music, has sustained some ideas, many others have become forgotten. The late Dr Prem Lata Sharma, well-known for her pioneering work in regenerating neglected ideas, states in this connection:

> The decline of the concept of '*sthāya*' in Sastraic and practical tradition is evident in Hindustani music from the complete loss of the terms associated with it and their replacement by popular and un-sastraic terms ... [38]

The need to revive the concepts of *sthāya* in Hindustani music is emphasized in this article and it remains to be seen how this point of view influences future trends in performance practice. At this time there is considerable talk in the West about an upsurge of energy giving rise to the renewal of different spiritual traditions. As we can observe from history, similar patterns of energy can affect different cultures at around the same time. It is not inconceivable, therefore, that some forms of Indian classical music might also experience the benefits of this upsurge of energy if the right quality of research were to be put into practice and not relegated to the realms of academic theory and speculation only.

However, studying the building blocks of a style based on improvisation is, in part, a process of 'innumerable small particles which coalesce'.[39] This is a principle which reminds one again of the pervasive influence of language, Sanskrit language, on musical evolution. The monumental work attributed to the grammarian, Pāṇini, relates to the roots and structures of the Sanskrit language, revealing clearly how it is indeed made up of 'small structures which coalesce'. Linguistically, one could talk about three levels in terms of a phonetic level, a phonemic level and a morphemic level. Pāṇini's work shows the laws by which a word develops from a seed to a root to a stem to a fully inflected word, and then the part that it plays in a sentence. Careful study of a musical rendition, especially in the opening slow improvised *ālāpa* section, can be heard to evolve in a similarly morphological way. This shows that the accumulation of small structures is an influence which, surely, cannot be ignored. However, it is not only a coming-together of small structures which accounts for the music as a whole, but additional qualities, such as intonation, *uccāra* and *kāku*, whose cumulative effect is responsible for the general impression generated by a particular style.

Kāku may best be described in terms of linguistic influence for it is a special concept, described by Bharata and borrowed from the theory of dramatic recitation, referring to vocal inflection as a result of the emotional content of the words being spoken. In musical terms it can be said to mean emotional colour or timbre. It is a 'skilful modulation of the voice', and 'is perhaps the key device by which music is instilled into the singer's own being on the one hand, and works up appeal and effects for the listener, on the other'.[40] We can also make the connection here between *kāku* and prosody, the musical and emotional content in language which resides in the domain of the right brain hemisphere as was discussed in Chapter 4. Later, six types of *kāku* are described by Śārṅgadeva;[41] however, the origins of the idea embodied in the term *kāku* existed long before this work. We should refer once again to the *Yājñavalkya Śikṣā*, a phonetic manual which describes a language very much older than that current in the thirteenth century, where subtle shades of aural colour required for correct pronunciation of *mantras* are described in some detail.[42] The influence of language on music is pervasive and, while the term *kāku* is a linguistic expression from an older terminology, it could equally be applied to the term *uccāra* used in contemporary parlance.

Uccāra is a term which can be interpreted as 'utterance', 'pronunciation' or even 'declaration'.[43] It can also mean 'articulation'.[44] These are all terms which one would normally associate with speech. To the practising musician they refer to the proper expression of the tones of a *rāga* so that the *rāga* identity is clearly indicated. This is understood to include correct intonation of each and every *svara* of the *rāga*, both in pitch and expression. Thus, there is an aesthetic aspect:

> Ucchāra is the manner of utterance. This is surely important. There is a world of difference between a svara that is merely thrust, abruptly and full-blown, into listening, and one that is quietly breathed into silence, and made to crystallize gradually.[45]

There are echoes here of the discussion on *svara sādhanā*, for:

> ... it is when *svara sādhanā* is practised relentlessly that it produces a curiously miraculous quality in the *svara* of the musical scales as an inaudible resonance of intent that shines through each utterance which enriches the passages of song with a strange inevitability.[46]

There is a difference between the long-held tones when they are sung by a musician who has training but who has never done *sādhanā*.

> The same waiting on a long held syllable of one whose music has emerged from *sādhanā* makes every instance of the syllable throb with meaning [47]

This, too, is *uccāra* but a refinement of it. While the term appears to be a contemporary idea in usage and description, it is in fact an old idea. Something similar is described in Nārada's early work. The hymns (*sāmans*) of the *Sāma Veda*, it is stated, should be sung smoothly as the path of a hawk circling in the sky. The transitions between syllables are to be rendered both accurately and smoothly but without too obvious a connection; just as there is no visible line of division between shade and sunlight. One should not attack the syllables with excessive force, nor with pressure of the tongue, nor too loudly, nor with a wavering voice. Both the *Śikṣā* of Nārada and of Yājñavalkya use the same colourful analogy to describe how the syllables should be recited – as a tigress carries her cubs with her teeth, neither biting them nor holding them so loosely that they fall – for many parts of the mouth are involved, as was explained in Chapter 2. The intensity of the melodic line should be sustained, just as it should in contemporary rendition.

The perception and feeling for *svara* is of the essence in listening to and appreciating the masters of Indian music. One could say, too, that such *svaras* require preparation, just as a dancer prepares an important gesture, just as there exists an 'up beat' in Western music, so too does the singer announce the *svara*. This is often done with the use of prefixes and suffixes. One could say that a single tone can have a back and a front. It may be introduced by something as transient and imperceptible as a subtle hint of an adjacent tone (a *kaṇa svara*) or by something more fully fledged such as a small cluster of tones, an *alaṅkāra*, or in some styles by a small *tāna*, nowadays frequently referred to as a *kaṭkā* or *murkī*.[48] Different variations of this concept of the 'up beat' can be heard depending on the style of singing in question, but the origin is likely to have been influenced by those shades of Vedic song which may be detected in the frequently heard play around the tonic, which takes the form of the tone immediately below and the tone immediately above (*sa*, *ni* and *re*) at the commencement of an *ālāpa*. Here the three accents of recitation are reflected in musical form and, as such, constitute an energy generating point for the rest of the *rāga* performance. This cluster of three tones can also be heard working at the level of a prefix to a tone, being a speeded-up version of the three accents.

Whatever the derivation, just as the beginning of a tone should not be abrupt, so it should not end abruptly. A suffix similar to its prefix may also be heard. It can hardly escape notice that a frequently heard musical suffix, certainly in the Ḍāgar style of *dhrupada* rendition, is one which is rhythmically identical to that heard in a multitude of four-syllable verbs, rhythmically *laghu, guru, laghu laghu* (short, long, short, short). It is by far the most frequently used cadence in both the *Gāyatrī* and *Anuṣṭubh* metres of the *Ṛg Veda* and is yet another indication of the pervasive influence of language.[49]

Such affixes to the main tone not only adorn but enrich the overall sonority of the tone so that the whole is conceived of as a single idea. Thus, the whole complex communicates a musical idea in the same way that a figure of speech does in literature. This, again, reinforces the idea of a fundamental connection in the Indian music tradition with 'the word' as the essence of conceptualization, that is unlike the evolution of other musical traditions.

The examples given are in *rāga Darbārī Kāṇaḍā*. There are many features essential to the proper performance of this dignified and majestic *rāga* but for the purposes of this discussion it is sufficient to know that the tone material for this *rāga* has all seven notes present in ascent and in descent with the third, sixth and seventh tones flattened.[50] The first seven examples (a–g), showing the gradual build-up of the sonic dimensions of a single tone around the tonic *Sa*, could be characteristic of a Ḍāgar style *dhrupada* performance, while the last two examples (h and i) would be more characteristic of a performance of *khayāl*. The choice of 'C' as the tonic in Western notation is for convenience of notation only; in practice, the singer chooses his or her own tonic pitch.

The actual sound produced by the singer is very much more curvaceous than any linear representation can convey. The sense of continuity, of one tone merging with another, is a feature which permeates Indian music. This feeling for the euphonic blending of sounds has been discussed already in the context of Sanskrit language and the pervasive use of *sandhi* and then again in a musical context in the relationship between *śruti* and *svara*. Before Mataṅga's philosophical expositions on the subject around the ninth century AD, there was already some evidence for this idea in the *Nāradīya Śikṣā* where there is fragmentary reference to sustained tones in the use of the term *tāna*, meaning to 'spread' or 'stretch'. This word could refer to the spreading out of a melodic idea in a series of tones or to the extending of a single tone. The concept is also present in the *upagāna* employed in *Sāman* music in which the syllable '*ho*' was sung continuously in the lower register.[51] Moreover, at a more subtle level, the method of recitation itself, if done properly, is intended to create a sustained resonance at the level of the navel, a connection ultimately with *Om*, the causal sound and the level of *paśyantī*. Although drone instruments do not feature in Bharata's theatre ensemble, the technique of recitation has been said to herald the subsequent use of a sustained drone which has been ubiquitous in Indian classical music since the sixteenth or seventeenth century when the starting tone for all *rāgas*, *Sa* of the system of *sargama*, became a fixed idea.[52] Thus we may wonder at the threads of continuity which pervade the practice of North Indian classical music.

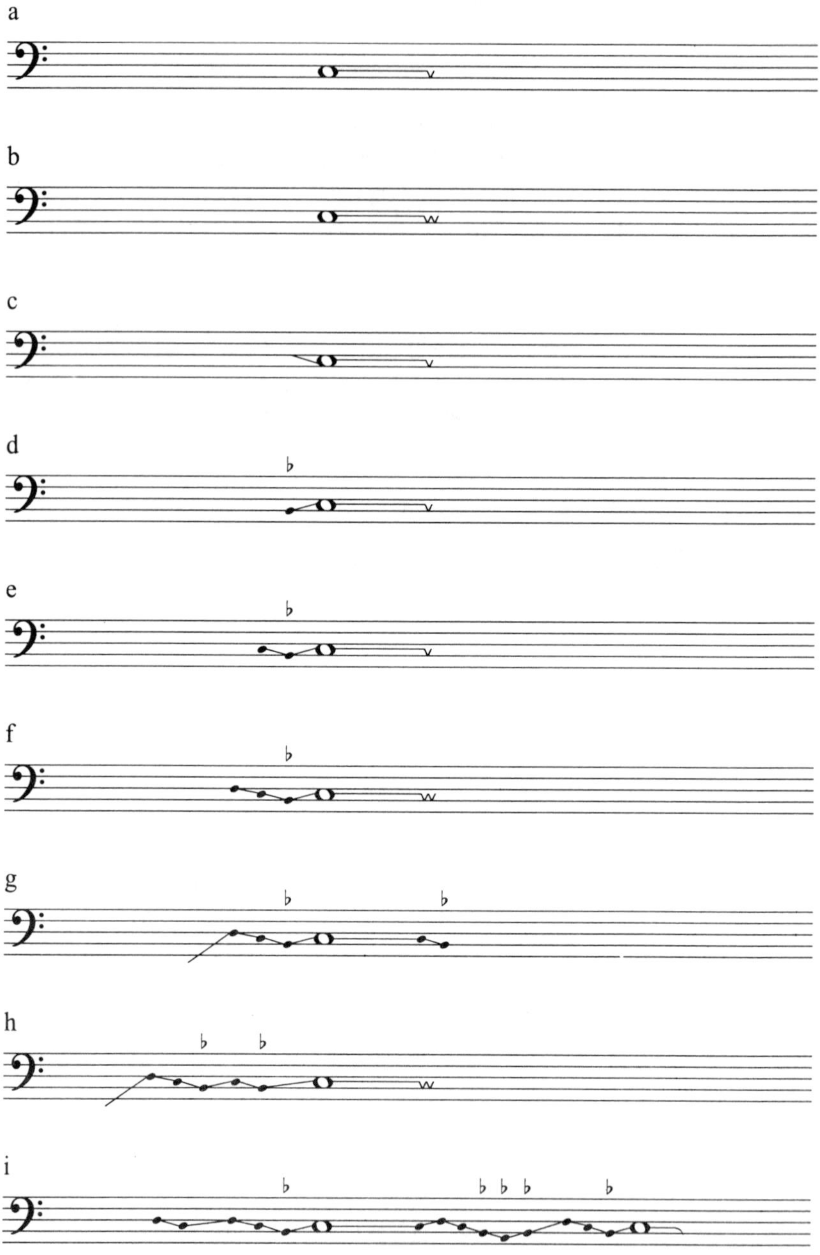

Figure 7.1 Music notation showing prefixes and suffixes to a main tone

Notes

1 Khan, 1977, p. 1.
2 See 'The Ear of the Heart – Levels of Sound' in Chapter 1. There is a relationship between the four *śaktis* (energies) of sound and hearing depending on the calibre of the musician and the capacity of the listener.
3 *Nāradīya Śikṣā*, 1.2.1.
4 *Yājñavalkya Śikṣā*, 1:26-28 and 2:82-84.
5 Rowell, 1992, p. 304
6 Bharata, *Nātya Śāstra*, 27:49-52.
7 *Nātya Śāstra,* 27:55-56.
8 See Chapter 3; Also Strangways, p. 246.
9 Monier-Williams, p. 348.
10 *Nātya Śāstra*, 29:44-70.
11 *Nāradīya Śikṣā*, 1.2.11.
12 Chaitanya B. Deva (1981), *The Music of India : A Scientific Study*, Munshiram Manoharlal Pvt. Ltd., New Delhi p. 92.
13 *Nāradīya Śikṣā*, 1.7.9.
14 The word *saptaka* meaning a collection of seven tones, is used in preference to the word 'octave' as the eighth tone is only a repetition of the first tone at a higher frequency.
15 Deva, 1981, p. 101.
16 A. Ranade (1990), *Keywords and Concepts*, Promilla and Co., New Delhi p. 52. It has another meaning depending on the perceived etymology of the word for it can also mean 'to adorn, decorate or grace'.
17 This is a much quoted reference in Bharata's *Nātya Śāstra*, 29:75.
18 Sangeet Natak Akademi, Delhi, Tapes Nos. 2103 and 2104, 31.7.78, Dr P.L. Sharma.
19 This subject is discussed in depth by Abhinavagupta and Mataṅga. Also Sangeet Natak Akademi, Tapes Nos. 2103 and 2104, 31.7.78, Dr P.L. Sharma.
20 Lath, p. 305.
21 Sharma and Shringy, 1991, p. 237.
22 N A. Jairazbhoy (1961), 'Svaraprastāra in North Indian Classical Music', *Bulletin of the School of Oriental and African Studies*, vol. 24, pp. 307-325.
23 Sharma and Shringy, 1989, p. 173.
24 Sharma and Shringy, 1989, p. 172.
25 Deva, 1981, p. 84.
26 L. Meyer (1956), *Emotion and Meaning in Music*, The University of Chicago Press, Chicago, p. 205.
27 Sharma and Shringy, 1989, p. 172, and also McIntosh, 1993.
28 Lath, p. 310.
29 *Gāndharva* is the ancient name for what later became known as *mārga* (music of the Path) when used in the context of *deśī* (regional music). This 'music of the Path' may originally have been the music of *mantras*, sound patterns meant

expressly for a specific occultic function, bound by strict rules. In the course of time any music governed by a set of specific rules was referred to as *mārgi sangīta*. Moreover, music writers tended to describe music previous to themselves as 'music of the Path' and their own music as *deśī* even though it also had a 'grammar', for 'regional music' did not mean it was folk music.

30 Solveig McIntosh (1993), *Gamaka and Alaṅkāra:Concepts of Vocal Ornamentation*, unpub. PhD, City University, London.

31 Sharma and Shringy, 1991, pp. 281-91.

32 Sharma and Shringy, 1991, p. 159.

33 The tendency since the latter half of the nineteenth century towards classification on the basis of scales is a limited interpretation of the Śāstraic tradition and in consequence omits important aspects of *rāga* conceptualization.

34 Sharma and Shringy, 1989, p.179. Examples of *svarakāku* would be the *āndolita* on *Ga komal* in *rāga Darbāri Kānāḍā* or the special intonation of *Ri komal* in *rāga Bhairava*. See also McIntosh, 1993.

35 S.N. Ratanjankar, (1952), 'Rāga Expression in Hindustani Music', *Journal of Madras Academy,* vol. XXIII, pp. 54-63.

36 S.N. Ratanjankar, (1951), 'Rāgas in Hindustani Music', *Journal of Madras Academy,* vol. XXII, pp. 97-105.

37 Howard, 1986, p. 224.

38 Prem Lata Sharma (1965), The Concept of Sthāya in Saṇgītaśāstra,' *Indian Music Journal,* vol. 3, pp. 29-35.

39 Deshpande, p. 30.

40 Saxena, p. 162.

41 Sharma and Shringy, 1989, p. 179.

42 *Yājñavalkya Śikṣā*, 3:59-80.

43 Ranade, p. 93.

44 Ranade, p. 53.

45 Saxena, p. 162.

46 Menon, 1999, p. 60.

47 Menon, p. 60.

48 McIntosh, 1993.

49 for example, *kariṣyasi* (thou shalt undertake) – short, long, short, short or *laghu, guru, laghu, laghu*.

50 McIntosh, 1993.

51 Tarlekar, p. 39.

52 Chaitanya B. Deva, (1967), 'The Emergence of the Drone in Indian Music' in *Psychoacoustics of Music and Speech*, Madras Music Academy, pp. 58-86.

Epilogue

Finally, it may be asked: what is the purpose of so much knowledge about the evolution of a musical art? Several indications have been given throughout the book and an attempt has been made to address some of the questions outlined in the opening Preface. The antiquity of Indian music and, at the same time, the sense of continuity of tradition is impressive. The need to enliven any investigation into the realm of knowledge by observing contemporary musical practice is clearly important. This highlights the requirement that elements of rendition, which have their roots in much older forms of music, should be re-examined and respected. Enquiry also makes clear that the practice of classical music in India cannot be separated from its heritage of philosophic, esoteric and linguistic influences. But not only this. Observation and exploration of such influences strongly suggest that a revival of ancient forms of music which existed within the Indian tradition should be stimulated so that contemporary practice may be enriched as it continues to evolve and move forward. For music is not about theory; most of what is recorded as theory is abstracted from practice and what is heard in practice has to do with the emotional and aesthetic content. In an oral tradition such as has existed in Northern Indian classical music much depends on the creative capacity of the artist. The purpose of knowledge, therefore, is to enable the listener and participator to think more specifically about what is heard, adding both substance and meaning to feelings. To enquire into the nature of some of the oldest music which has survived and to study the written literature which still exists is not mere academia; it reveals aspects of contemporary music practice and casts a light which may show the way forward.

Appendix 1
Guide to Pronunciation

Position 1

a	guttural vowel, as in hut
ā	elongation of voiced guttural vowel, as in father
k	voiceless guttural, as in kin
kh	voiceless, aspirated guttural, as in inkhorn*
g	voiced guttural, as in got
gh	voiced, aspirated guttural, as in aghast
ṅ	guttural nasal sound, nearest English equivalent, sing*
h	voiced guttural sound, as in hat

Position 2

i	palatal vowel, as in hit
ī	elongation of voiced palatal vowel, as in meet
c	voiceless palatal, as in cheer
ch	voiceless palatal, as in Churchill*
j	voiced palatal, as in jug
jh	aspirated voiced palatal, as in hedgehog*
ñ	nasal palatal sound, nearest English equivalent impinge
y	voiced palatal semivowel, as in yes
ś	voiceless palatal sibilant, nearest English equivalent shoe

Position 3

ṛ	voiced cerebral vowel, nearest English equivalent rich
ṝ	elongation of voiced cerebral vowel, no English equivalent
ṭ	voiceless cerebral sound, nearest equivalent sound trip
ṭh	voiceless aspirated cerebral sound, as in anthill*
ḍ	voiced cerebral sound, as in drag
ḍh	voiced aspirated cerebral sound, as in redhaired*
ṇ	voiced nasal cerebral sound, as in nobody
r	voiced cerebral sound, as in rag
ṣ	voiceless cerebral sibilant, as in ship

Position 4

ḷ	voiced dental vowel, no English equivalent
t	voiceless dental sound, as in top

th	voiceless aspirated dental sound, as in nuthook*
d	voiced dental sound, as in dog
dh	voiced aspirated dental sound, as in adhere*
n	nasal voiced dental sound, as in net
l	voiced dental sound, as in love
s	voiceless sibilant sound, as in sun

Position 5

u	voiced labial vowel, as in put
ū	elongated voiced labial vowel, as in cool
p	voiceless labial sound, as in pull
ph	voiceless aspirated labial sound, as in uphill*
b	voiced labial sound, as in bag
bh	voiced aspirated labial sound, as in abhor*
m	voiced labial sound, as in milk
v	voiced semivowel as in vogue or wing

e	as in acre
ai	as in aisle
o	as in ochre
au	as in outer

* Examples taken from M. Monier-Williams, *Sanskrit-English Dictionary*, Motilal Banarsidass Publishers Pvt Ltd, Delhi.

Appendix 2

The Sanskrit Alphabet

Position 1 Guttural		Position 2 Palatal		Position 3 Cerebral		Position 4 Dental		Position 5 Labial	
अ	a	इ	i	ऋ	ṛ	ऌ	ḷ	उ	u
आ	ā	ई	ī	ॠ	ṝ	ॡ	ḷ	ऊ	ū
क	k	च	c	ट	ṭ	त	t	प	p
ख	kh	छ	ch	ठ	ṭh	थ	th	फ	ph
ग	g	ज	j	ड	ḍ	द	d	ब	b
घ	gh	झ	jh	ढ	ḍh	ध	dh	भ	bh
ङ	ṅ	ञ	ñ	ण	ṇ	न	n	म	m
ह	h	य	y	र	r	ल	l	व	v
		श	ś	ष	ṣ	स	s		

Guttural and Palatal

ए e ऐ ai

Guttural and Labial

ओ o औ au

Anusvāra

· ṁ

Visarga

: ḥ

Appendix 3
Relevant Literature

The Vedas are ancient texts consisting of *mantras* which may also be referred to as hymns or 'sacred songs'. The word literally means 'knowledge' from the root *vid*, 'to know'. Vedas were not composed or recorded. They were revealed knowledge (*śrutis*) communicated from the Divine (*brahman*) to the ancient seers (*ṛṣis*) and consequently referred to as *apauruṣeya* (without an ascribed human author). The four Vedas are known as the *Ṛg Veda*, the *Yajur Veda*, the *Sāma Veda* and the *Artharva Veda*. The first three are thought to refer to the three paths to liberation: the path of knowledge (*jñāna*) identified with the *Ṛg Veda*, of devotion (*bhakti*) the *Sāma Veda* and of action (*karma*) the *Yajur Veda*. Each of the Vedas has two parts, *saṃhitā* (hymns)and the *brāhmaṇas* (prayers or utterances of devotion). It is not known what proportion of the sacred songs which existed at that time were included in the four Vedas or what was lost.

The *saṁhitā* consist of *mantras* or incantations used in sacrifices. These *mantras* are difficult to interpret without commentaries and, consequently, the *brāhmaṇas* set out to explain the hymns and the rituals. The part of the Vedas which deals with rituals is referred to as *karma kaṇḍa*.

Vedic literature also includes knowledge which is expounded in the *āraṇyakas* (forest treatises) and the *upaniṣads*. A narrow definition of Veda means the *mantras* (*saṃhitā*) alone, but a broader understanding includes the *brāhmaṇas, āraṇyakas* and *upaniṣads*.

The *āranyakas* are what is known as *Vedānta* (end of the Vedas) and are appendices to the *brāhmaṇas*. They contain secret codes relating to sacrifices, mystical and symbolic, and were intended to be learnt only in the forest and not in the villages. They represent a stage of life which takes place after purification through the practice of Vedic rites.

The *upaniṣads* comprise profound and sacred teachings imparted to the disciple who sits at the feet of his *guru*. They are rich in philosophical thought and represent the culmination of teachings set forth in the *saṁhitās*, the *brāhmaṇas* and the *āraṇyakas*, throwing light on the meaning and purpose of the aforesaid. There are many, but the following are relevant to this book: the *Bṛhadāraṇyaka*, the *Chāndogya Upaniṣad*, *Taittirīya Upaniṣad*, *Kena Upaniṣad*, *Katha Upaniṣad*, *Iśā Upaniṣad*, *Māṇḍūkya Upaniṣad*.

Post Vedic literature is referred to as the *Sūtra* Period. These were manuals of instructions in the form of brief rules written as aphorisms, hence the term *sūtra* or thread. The earliest *sūtras* were the 'Limbs of the Vedas' (*Vedāṅgas*); they were six in number consisting of phonetics (*śikṣā*), ritual or religious practice (*kalpa*), grammar (*vyākaraṇa*), etymology (*nirukta*), metrics (*chandas*) and astronomy (*jyotīsa*). The best known are Yāska's etymology (*Nirukta*) and Pāṇini's grammar (*Vyākaraṇa*). They were regarded as 'traditional knowledge' (*smṛti*) rather than 'revealed knowledge' (*śruti*).

The most important of the phonetic manuals (*śikṣās*) are considered to be the *Yājñavalkya Śikṣā* for *Yajur Veda*, *Nāradīya Śikṣā* for *Sāma Veda* and the *Śikṣā* of Pāṇini. They cover such topics as pronunciation of *mantras*, gestures (*mudrās*), theory and other items of practical advice for the intending student. These phonetic manuals, like most other early Indian writings, are compilations consisting of material from different authors and representing different periods of history. The six principal topics of phonetic theory outlined in the *Taittirīya Upaniṣad* are *varṇa*, the individual sounds and letters; *svara*, accents, pitches, vowels; *mātrā*, metre, syllable, quantity, duration; *bala*, dynamics, resonance, articulatory force; *sāma*, performance as a whole; and *santāna*, the euphonic laws connecting syllables.

The *prātiśākhyas* are reference manuals for detailed examination of phonetic matters as they pertain to a particular school (*śākhā*) of a Veda, namely:

Ṛg Veda	*Ṛk Prātiśākhya*
Sāma Veda	*Ṛk tantra-vyākaraṇa*
Black *Yajur Veda*	*Taittirīya Prātiśākhya*
White *Yajur Veda*	*Vajasaneyi or Kātyāyanīya Prātiśākhya*
Atharva Veda	*Atharva Prātiśākhya*

There may, at one time, have been many more *prātiśākhyas* but only six have remained available. Many more *śikṣās* exist and their scope applies, to a considerable extent, to the *prātiśākhyas* as well. It is generally thought that the original *śikṣās* are probably older than the *prātiśākhyas*, but most of the extant manuals appear to have been compiled at a date later than the few surviving *prātiśākhyas*. It is said that if the *śikṣā* and the *prātiśākhya* are at variance, then the *prātiśākhya* is the more authoritative.

Glossary

ābhoga	the final section in chant or in a *prabandha.*
adrṣta phalla	unseen result or 'fruit'.
āghāta	onset, attack.
akāra	to sing a vowel sound.
ākāśa	ether, space, the medium of sound.
akṣara	syllable.
alaṅkāra	literally 'that which makes sufficient, making clear or intelligible', hence melodic pattern or ornament.
ālāpa	non-metrical exposition of a *rāga* at the beginning of a composition or performance.
alpatva	a tone which occurs frequently.
aṁśa	the tonic or sonant tone, the most prominent tone in a *jāti* or *grāmarāga.*
āndolana	'oscillating' at slow speed.
āndolita	'oscillated' at slow speed.
aṅga	'limb', a part of anything, often meaning a formal component.
anibaddha	unregulated.
anudātta	a 'lowered' accent in Vedic recitation.
anunāsika	a nasal sound made through the mouth and the nose.
anuraṇana	resonance (as a result of '*āghāta*').
anusvāra	a nasal sound using the nose only.
āroha	ascending order of tones.
Aṣṭādhyāyī	literally 'eight meditations', Pāṇini's Sanskrit grammar *c* 600 BC.
avaroha	descending order of tones.
āyatā	'stretched' or extended.
bahutva	prevalence of a tone.
bāni	stylistic school.
bhakti	devotion.
bīn	considered the most ancient and revered of musical instruments in India, a form of stick zither, also called *vīṇā.*
bindu	'drop', a point or very fine focus.
bolbant	rhythmical play with the words in *dhrupada.*
Brahman (n)	a philosophical term applied to the Absolute of the Universe, the highest principle. Nominative singular form used is *Brahma.*

Brahman (m) — a term used for the Creator of a Solar System. Nominative singular form used is *Brahmā*.

cakra — wheel, energy centres along the spine.
chandas — meter
chāyā — image, reflection.

deśi — music which entertains the people, regional, provincial.
dha, dhaivata — the sixth scale degree.
dhātu — roots in Sanskrit from which words are derived, a component of a *prabandha.*
dhrupada — the oldest surviving form of classical vocal music in Northern India.
dhruvā — a song sung during the performance of a play.
dhvani — reverberating sound and its implications.
diptā — bright, brilliant.

ga, gāndhāra — the third scale degree.
gamaka — a melodic transition between tones or ornamentation in general. It can also mean a heavy 'shake' from one or a number of tones.
gāna — the style of incidental music for the ancient theatre, the dramatic songs.
gandharva — refers to a celestial musician.
gāndharva — broadly refers to music in general, used specifically it means a genre of ritual music performed during the prelude to a play.
gāthās — songs sung for ceremonies and festivals.
ghum — an internalizing nasal sound with no specific meaning, a Vedic *anunāsika.*
gītā — song, art music.
gītaka — a name for a composition performed during the ritual prelude to a play.
gīti — text setting or style in general.
graha — a beginning.
grāma — a collection of tones, a scale system.
grāma rāga — a scalar mode.
guru — a measure of relatively long duration in music or poetry, a teacher.

iḍā — one of the three principal *nāḍīs* originating at the base of the spine and terminating at the left nostril. See *piṇgalā* and *suṣumnā.*

jāti	a melodic species, relating to one of the ancient mode classes, parent scale from which *rāgas* are derived.
kāku	intonation in dramatic recitation, vocal inflection, timbre.
kampana	'shaking' or 'vibrating'.
kampita	a melodic quiver or oscillation, 'shaken' or 'vibrated'.
kaṇa	'particle', an articulatory tone varying in degree of audibility.
karuṇā	mournful.
kaṭkā	an ornamental configuration around a tone.
khayāl	a genre of North Indian classical vocal music.
kirtana	singing the praises of God.
komala	a tone which has been lowered.
kūṭa tāna	a *tāna* whose sequence of tones is not 'straight'.
laghu	a measure of short duration in music and poetry.
lakṣaṇa	a distinguishing mark or feature, a finesse.
laya	the process of calibrating time referring to tempo or to an unmetred pulse.
laykārī	rhythmical play with words and syllables.
ma, madhyama	the fourth scale degree, moderate in terms of the five *śrutis*.
madhyamā	subtle level of sound.
madhya	medium, middle.
maṅdra	low, the lowest register.
mantra	Sanskrit formulae used in recitation, the hymns of the Vedas.
mārga	'path', ancient musical system.
mātṛkā	mother energies emanating from the Absolute Creator.
mīṇḍa	refers to specific and non-specific glides.
mṛdu	soft.
mudrā	a hand gesture in Vedic recitation (and also later in dance).
mūrchanā	'expanding, spreading', as in the rotations of the basic scales, sets of octave species.
murkī	a fast ornamental configuration.
nāda	'causal sound', subtle resonance, the metaphysical theory of sound.
nāḍīs	subtle channels of energy in the human body.
nāṭya	drama.
ni, niṣāda	the seventh scale degree.

nibaddha regulated.
note a pitch which is notated.
nyāsa the final tone.

pa, pañcama the fifth scale degree.
pada 'word' relating to text in general or a passage of music set to a meaningful text (as opposed to nonsense syllables).
padapāṭha word-by-word recitation.
pāda a portion of a larger unit, usually a quarter.
paltā *alaṁkāra.*
paṇḍit clever, learned, a scholar, honorific title.
paśyantī the causal state of sound.
piṇgalā one of the three principal *nāḍīs* originating at the base of the spine and terminating at the right nostril. See *iḍā,* and *suṣumnā.*
pluta a protracted duration in music or three time measures in language.
prabandha an art-song, lit. 'well combined' or 'well-knit'.
pracaya when a 'lowered' sound (*anudātta*) follows a *svarita* accent it is called *pracaya* or *ekasvara.*
pradeśa the span from tip of first finger to tip of thumb when stretched apart, a unit of measurement.
prāṇa breath, life-current.
prastāra permutations.
pūrvaṅga lower half of the octave, first tetrachord.
pūrvaraṅga the ritual prelude to a play.

rāga tonal scheme, melodic framework, 'colour', 'atmosphere'.
raṅga a *ghum* sound of two measures.
ri, ṛṣabha the second scale degree.
ṛṣis sages, seers.
rūpa form.
rūpaka an alternative term for *prabandha* with reference to its poetic content.

sa, ṣaḍja the first scale degree, tonic.
śabda word or sound which has meaning.
śakti feminine energy, vibrations.
sāmān a *Sāma Vedic* chant or hymn.
saṁhitāpāṭha recitation with words joined according to the laws of *sandhi.*

saṃvādī a consonant tone, a tone in perfect fifth or fourth relation with the *vādi.*

sandhi junction point, euphonic combination. The word *sandhi* is made up of *sam*, a prefix meaning 'together' and *dhi* from the root *dhā* meaning 'to hold', *saṃdhi.* These two syllables in combination illustrate the process of *sandhi.*

saṅgati two notes which are associated with one another within a mode, possibly involving frequent movement between them.

saṅgīta art-music, comprising vocal music, instrumental music and dance.

Saṅgīta Ratnākara literally 'Ocean of Music'.

saṅgītaśāstra treatises on music.

saptaka 'the set of seven' degrees of the heptatonic scale, or intervals of the octave.

sargama seven solfa syllables.

śāstras treatises.

śikṣā phonetic manual, ancient source information on music.

ślokas a metrical couplet.

spanda primary conscious vibration, a term used in Kashmir Śaivism.

sphoṭa a sound in the form of a word which 'flashes' on the mind when uttered.

śruti audible sound, microtones; (i) intonation in general; (ii) the twenty-two divisions of the octave; (iii) the five *śruti* tonal qualities.

sthāna register, location.

sthāya a phrase with embellishments.

śuddha pure, natural position of the tones.

sūkta well spoken, a Vedic hymn.

suṣumnā one of the three principal *nāḍīs* covering the area from the base of the spine to the top of the corpus callosum. See *īḍā,* and *piṇgalā.*

sūtra (sūt) thread, formula, axiom.

svara vowel, syllable, musical tone, a term for pitch in general, one of the seven scale degrees.

svarita intermediate accent or tone in Vedic recitation.

tāna a pentatonic or hexatonic mūrchanā, a variant of one of the basic scales, a rapid sequence of notes.

tānpurā plucked stringed instrument of long-necked lute variety which serves as an accompanying drone.

tone a sound which is sensed, heard and manifest or performed.

uccāra	correct rendering in intonation and expression.
udātta	a 'raised' accent in Vedic recitation.
upagāna	a musical prelude, a preparatory tune, a short *ālāpa* before the main piece.
upaniṣads	Vedānta, final expression of the Vedas, represent ultimate Truth
uttaraṅga	upper tetrachord (*pa* to *sa*).
vāc	personified in the Vedas as the goddess of speech and music.
vādi	the sonant tone in a scale, equivalent to *aṃśa.*
vaikharī	manifest, articulated sound.
vānī	(***bānī***), a school of *dhrupada.*
varṇa	a melodic contour or movement.
vāyu	air, a field of operation.
vikṛta	distorted, impure, modified. In Vedic recitation, word division, repetition and patterning.
vīṇā	(***bīna***), a stringed instrument.
viśrānta	reposed, rested or ceased from.
vistāra	spreading, expansion, extent, becoming large.
yajña	ritual actions or oblations during the act of worship.

Bibliography

Agrawala, V.S. (1953), *India as Known to Pāṇini*, University of Lucknow, Lucknow.

Allen, W. Sidney (1953), *Phonetics in Ancient India*, Oxford University Press, London.

Aṣṭādhyāyī of Pāṇini, Śrīsā Chandra Vasu trans. (1891), Motilal Banarsidass, Delhi.

Ballantyne, James (1995 ed.) *The Laghukaumudī*, A Sanskrit Grammar by Varadarāja, Motilal Banarsidass Pvt Ltd. Delhi.

Beck, Guy L. (1995), *Sonic Theology, Hinduism and Sacred Sound*, Motilal Banarsidass Publishers Pvt. Ltd, Delhi.

Bharata, *Nāṭyaśāstra of Bharatamuni, with the Commentary Abhinavabhāratī by Abhinavaguptācārya*, (1926-64), ed. M. Ramakrishna Kavi and J.S. Pade, Oriental Institute, Baroda.

Bharata, *The Nāṭyaśāstra, An English Translation with Critical Notes*, (1996), trans. Adya Rangacharya, Munshiram Manoharlal Publishers Pvt. Ltd, New Delhi.

Chetānanda, Swāmī (1991),'The Symphony of Life', in Don Campbell, ed. *Music Physician for Times to Come*, Quest Books, Theosophical Publishing House.

Dāthu Pāṭhaḥ, Shastri, J.L., ed. (1984), Motilal Banarsidass, Delhi.

Deshpande, V.H. (1973), *Indian Musical Traditions – An Aesthetic Study of the Gharanas in Hindustani Music*, Popular Prakashan, Bombay.

Deva, B. Chaitanya (1963), 'Transitive Elements in Music', *Nāda Rupa*.

Deva, B. Chaitanya (1967), 'The Emergence of the Drone in Indian Music', *Psychoacoustics of Music and Speech*, Madras Music Academy, Madras.

Deva, B. Chaitanya (1981), *The Music of India: A Scientific Study*, Munshiram Manoharlal Pvt. Ltd., New Delhi.

Fertman, Bruce (1994), 'The First Sound', *Direction. A Journal of the Alexander Technique*, vol. 2, no. 6.

Feuerstein, Georg, Subhash Kak and David Frawley (1999), *In Search of the Cradle of Civilization*, Motilal Banarsidass Publishers Pvt. Ltd, Delhi.

Freeman, Brian (1994), 'The Human Embryo's Use Of Its Self', *4th International Alexander Congress*, ed. David Garlick, Sydney, Australia.

Gambhirānanda, Swāmī, trans. (1980), *Kena Upaniṣad* with the commentary of Śaṅkarācārya, Advaita Ashrama, Calcutta.

Gambhirānanda, Swāmī, trans. (1980), *Taittirīya Upaniṣad* with the commentary of Śaṅkarācārya, Advaita Ashrama, Calcutta.

Gambhirānanda, Swāmī, trans. (1983), *Chāndogya Upaniṣad* with the commentary of Śaṅkarācārya, Advaita Ashrama, Calcutta.

Gambhirānanda, Swāmī (1995 ed.), *Māṇḍūkya Upaniṣad* with the commentary of Śaṅkarācārya, Advaita Ashrama, Calcutta.

Ghosh, Manmohan, ed. (1938), *Pāninīya Śikṣā*, Asian Humanities Press, Delhi.

Gray, J.E.B. (1959), 'An Analysis of Nambudiri Rgvedic Recitation and the Nature of Vedic Accent', *Bulletin of the School of Oriental and African Studies*, vol. 22, pp. 499-530.

Hopkins, Thomas J. (1971), *The Hindu Religious Tradition*, Dickinson, Encino, CA.

Howard, Wayne (1977), *Sāmavedic Chant*, Yale University Press, New Haven.

Howard, Wayne (1986), *Veda Recitation in Vārāṇasī*, Motilal Banarsidass Publishers Pvt. Ltd, Delhi.

Hume, R.E., ed. (2000), *Thirteen Principal Upanishads*, Oxford University Press, Delhi.

Jairazbhoy, N.A. (1961), 'Svaraprastāra in North Indian Classical Music', *Bulletin of the School of Oriental and African Studies*, vol. 24, pp. 307-325.

Jenny, Hans (1974), *Cymatics. Wave Phenomena, Vibrational Effects, Harmonic Oscillations with their Structure, Kinetics and Dynamics*, Basilius Presse, Basel, Switzerland.

Khan, Hazrat Inayat (1977), *Music*, Samuel Weiser, New York.

Khan, Hazrat Inayat (1972), *The Sufi Message*, 2nd edn, Barrie and Rockcliff, London, vol. 2.

Lannoy, Richard (1971), *The Speaking Tree: A Study of Indian Culture and Society*, Oxford University Press, London.

Lath, Mukund (1978), *A Study of Dattilam*, Impex, Delhi.

Macdonell, Arthur Anthony (1993), *A Vedic Grammar for Students*, Motilal Banarsidass Publishers Pvt. Ltd, Delhi.

Mascarô, J. (1994), Selected translations from the Chāndogya Upaniṣad, *The Upanishads*, Penguin Books, New Delhi.

Mataṅga (1992), *Bṛhaddeśī of Śrī Mataṅga Muni*, ed. Prem Lata Sharma, Indira Ghandi National Centre for the Arts, Delhi.

Menon, Raghava R. (1976), *The Sound of Indian Music: A Journey into Rāga*, Indian Book Company, New Delhi.

Menon, Raghava R. (1999), 'Dhvani, Nature and Culture of Sound', in *Proceedings of International Seminar on Sound 1994*, ed. S.C. Malik, Indira Gandhi National Centre for the Arts, New Delhi.

Meyer, L. (1956), *Emotion and Meaning in Music*, The University of Chicago Press, Chigaco.

McIntosh, Solveig (1993), 'Gamaka and Alaṅkāra: Concepts of Vocal Ornamentation', unpublished PhD thesis, City University, London.

McIntosh, Solveig (2001), 'Sanskrit', *The Bridge* No. 14, The Study Society, London.

Mishra, Vidhata (1972), *A Critical Study of Sanskrit Phonetics*, Chowkhamba Sanskrit Series Office, Vārāṇasī.

Monier-Williams, M. (1899), *A Sanskrit-English Dictionary*, Motilal Banarsidass Publishers Pvt. Ltd, Delhi.

Monier-Williams, M. (1978), *A Practical Grammar of the Sanskrit Language*, Oriental Books Reprint Corporation, Delhi.

Nader, Tony (1995), *Human Physiology*, Maharishi Vedic University, Vlodrop, The Netherlands.

Nārada (1986), *Nāradīya Śikṣā, with the Commentary of Bhaṭṭa Śobhākara*, trans. and ed. Usha R. Bhise, Bhandarkar Oriental Research Institute, Poona.

Nijenhuis, E. te (1992) *Saṅgītaśiromāṇī: Medieval handbook of Indian Music*, R.J. Brill, Leiden.

Padoux, André (1992), *Vāc. The Concept of the Word in Selected Hindu Tantras*, Sri Satguru Publications, Delhi.

Pāṇini, Aṣṭādhyāyī see Ballantyne, J.

Powers, H. (1980), 'India', in *New Grove Dictionary of Music and Musicians*, Macmillan, London, vol. 9.

Prajñānānanda, Swāmī (1973), *Historical Development of Indian Music*, Firma K.L. Mukhopadhyay, Calcutta.

Premalatha, V. (1985), *Music Through the Ages*, Sundeep Prakashan, Delhi.

Pūjyaśrī Chandraśekharendra Sarasvatī Svāmī (1995), *Hindu Dharma*, Bharatiya Vidya Bhavan, Bombay.

Ranade, A. (1990), *Keywords and Concepts*, Promilla and Co., New Delhi.

Ratanjankar, S.N. (1951), 'Rāgas in Hindustani Music', *Journal of Madras Academy*, vol. XXII, pp. 97-105.

Ratanjankar, S.N. (1952), 'Rāga Expression in Hindustani Music', *Journal of Madras Academy*, vol. XXIII, pp. 54-63.

Ratate, Vinayaka Ramchandra (1991), 'The Seeds of Dhrupad in Veda in the Form of "Stoma"', Dhrupad *Annual*, vol. 6, All India Kashi Raj Trust, Vārāṇasī.

Ṛg Veda Saṁhitā (2001 ed.) trans. H.H. Wilson and Bhāṣya of Sāyaṇācārya, vols. I-IV, Parimal Publications, Delhi.

Robertson, Paul (1996), *Music and the Mind*, Channel 4 Television, London.

Rowell, Lewis (1977), 'A Śikṣā for the Twiceborn', *Asian Music*, vol. 9, no. 1, pp. 72-94.

Rowell, Lewis (1992), *Music and Musical Thought in Early India*, The University of Chicago Press, Chicago.

Sachs, Curt (1943), *The Rise of Music in the Ancient World – East and West*, W.W. Norton, New York.

Śantānanda Saraswati (1975) 'Record of Audiences with Śantānanda Saraswatī, Śankarācārya of Jyotir Maṭh in Northern India from 1953-1980'. The Study Society, London.

Sanyal, R. and Widdess, R. (1994), 'Some Techniques of Layakārī in the Ḍāgar Tradition', *Dhrupad Annual*, vol. 9, All India Kashi Raj Trust, Vārāṇasī.

Saxena, S.K. (1981), 'Aesthetics of Hindustani Music', in *Aesthetical Essays*, Chanakya Publications, Delhi.

Shannatoff-Khalsa, D.S., and Yogi Bhajan (1989), *Sound Current Therapy and Self-Healing: The Ancient Science of Nad and Mantra Yoga*, The Khalsa Foundation for Medical Science, Del Mar, CA.

Sharma, Prem Lata, (1965), 'The Concept of Sthāya in Saṇgītaśāstra', *Indian Music Journal*, vol. 3, pp. 29-35.

Sharma, P.L. and Shringy, R.K. (1989), *Sangīta Ratnākara of Śārṇgadeva*, vol. 2, Munshiram Manoharlal Publishers Pvt. Ltd., New Delhi.

Sharma, P.L. and Shringy, R.K. (1991), *Sangīta Ratnākara of Śārṇgadeva*, vol. 1, Munshiram Manoharlal Publishers Pvt. Ltd, New Delhi.

Sharma, Prema Lata, ed. (1992), *Bṛhaddeśi of Mataṅga Muni*, Indira Ghandi National Centre for the Arts, Kalāmūlaśāstra series vol. 1, pp. 1-13.

Sharma, Prema Lata (2000), *Indian Aesthetics and Musicology*, Amnaya Prakasana, Vārānasī.

Shastri, J.L., ed. (1984), *Dāthu Pāṭhaḥ*, Motilal Banarsidass, Delhi.

Shringy, R.K. (1972), 'The Concept of Sruti as related to Svara – A Textual and Critical Study', *Journal of Madras Academy*, vol. XLIII, pp. 111-128.

Shlain, Leonard (1998), *The Alphabet Versus The Goddess*, Allen Lane, The Penguin Press, London.

Singh, Thakur Jaideva (1994), *Bhāratiya Saṇgīta kā Itihāsa*, Sangeet Research Academy, Calcutta.

Singh, Thakur Jaideva (1995), *Indian Music*, Sangeet Research Academy, Calcutta.

Srivastava, Indurama (1980), *Dhrupada*, Motilal Banarsidass Publishers Pvt. Ltd, Delhi.

Strangways, A.H. Fox (1994), *The Music of Hindostan*, Munshiram Manoharlal Pvt. Ltd, New Delhi.

Śukla Yajur Veda Saṃhitā, Wāsudev Shāstrī Paṇsikar, ed. (1912), pub. Tukaram Javaji, Bombay.

Swāmī, Rāma (1978), *Living with the Himalayan Masters*, The Himalayan Institute of Yoga Science and Philosophy, Honesdale, Pennsylvania, USA.

Swāmī, Madhavānanda, trans. (1934), *Bṛhadāranyaka Upaniṣad*, Advaita Ashrama, Calcutta.

Tarlekar, G.H. (1995), *Sāman Chants: In Theory and Present Practice*, Sri Satguru Publications, Delhi.

The Study Society, 'Record of Audiences with Śantānanda Saraswatī, Śankarācārya of Jyotir Maṭh in Northern India from 1953-1980', London.

Tomatis, Alfred A. (1991), *The Conscious Ear: My Life of Transformation Through Listening*, Station Hill Press Inc., New York.

Widdess, D.R. (1980), 'The Kuḍumiyāmalai Inscription: a source of early Indian music notation', *Musica Asiatica*, vol. 2, pp. 115-50.

Widdess, D.R. (1994), *Rāgas of Early Indian Music: Modes, Melodies and Musical Notations from the Gupta period to c.1250,* The Clarendon Press, Oxford.

Yājñavalkya Śikṣā (1962), ed. Amaranaṭha Śastri-Sampadita, pub. Prakāśaka Dīkśita Kṛṣnacandra Sharma Pasupadiksvara, Vārāṇasī.

Index